What Experts Are Saying About
WINDOWS INTO THE A.D.D. MIND

This is an excellent book on ADD. State-of-the-art information for parents and professionals interested in the diagnosis and treatment of ADD in children and adults. Dr. Amen takes a lot of complex information and explains it simply and clearly. His experience with over 2500 ADD children, teens, adults and their families is integrated with a warmth and deep understanding gained from the existence of ADD within his own family.

The book is practical and the buyer gets a lot of understandable and usable current information for the money. I bought two copies -- one to keep and one to loan!

Harold Russell, PhD, Clinical Psychologist and Professor of Psychology, University of Texas, Galveston

WINDOWS INTO THE A.D.D. MIND is a book filled with hope, practical suggestions, and valuable information for children, adults and families faced with the everyday challenges of living with A.D.D. As an adult with A.D.D. I especially appreciate Dr. Amen's honesty, openness, and optimism in his search for workable solutions.

Milton Lucius, PhD, Clinical Psychologist, Editor of the ADD Referral Network

With WINDOWS INTO THE A.D.D. MIND Dr. Amen throws back the curtains and unlocks the shutters so we can see how the A.D.D.mind works, how the A.D.D. individual feels, and how those who live and work with A.D.D. people can help.

This book is an excellent resource for parents, teachers, and therapists. It provides very practical suggestions for parenting, classroom accommodations, and behavior management. It is one of the few resources that provides specific information on cognitive-behavioral techniques that challenge negative thinking and faulty beliefs. A.D.D. adults will appreciate the tips for managing life with A.D.D. successfully. Parents and physicians will benefit from the information on medications used to treat A.D.D.

Lisa Zottnick, M.S., Certified Educational Therapist

WINDOWS INTO THE A.D.D. MIND is a groundbreaking book. It is insightful and revelatory, affording genuine help to all persons with A.D.D. It is partic-ularly enlightening in its identification and analysis of A.D.D. in adults. Dr. Amen is a foremost authority on A.D.D. and this book will certainly enhance his reputation.

Mel Krantzler, Ph.D., author of Learning To Love Again. and Creative Divorce

Windows into the

A.D.D.

MIND

**Understanding And Treating
Attention Deficit Disorders
In The Everyday Lives Of
Children, Adolescents And Adults**

Daniel G. Amen, M.D.
Neuropsychiatrist

MindWorks Press
Fairfield, California 1995

MindWorks Press
2220 Boynton Avenue, Suite C
Fairfield, California 94533
(707) 429-7181

ISBN 1-886554-00-5
Cover Design by Lightbourne Images
Manufactured in the United States of America
9 8 7 6 5 4 3 2 1

Other Books By Dr. Amen

IMAGES INTO THE MIND:
A Radical New Look At Understanding and Changing Behavior
DON'T SHOOT YOURSELF IN THE FOOT
A Program To End Self-Defeating Behavior Forever
NEW SKILLS FOR FRAZZLED PARENTS
Superior Skills for Parenting Difficult Kids
HEALING THE CHAOS WITHIN
The Interaction Between A.D.D., Alcoholism
and Growing Up In an Alcoholic Home
MINDCOACH FOR KIDS
Teaching Kids and Teens To Think Positive and Feel Good
WOULD YOU GIVE TWO MINUTES A DAY
FOR A LIFETIME OF LOVE
TEN STEPS TO BUILDING VALUES WITHIN CHILDREN
A TEENAGER'S GUIDE TO A.D.D.

Confidentiality is essential to psychiatric practice. All case descriptions in this book, therefore, have
been altered to preserve the anonymity of my patients without distorting the essentials of their stories.

The advice offered in this book, although based on the author's experience with thousands of patients,
is not intended to be a substitue for the advice and counsel of your personal physician.

To my patients and their families, who have taught
me that things are not always as they seem.

Note:

In the book, I'll use the term ADD to refer to both attention deficit hyperactivity disorder, attention deficit disorder without hyperactivity, and the other subtypes of ADD. I will distinguish between the conditions in the text.

INTRODUCTION

"Try harder. If only you would try harder you'd do better." This is a common statement heard by children, teens and adults who have Attention Deficit Disorder (ADD). Unfortunately, it is false. The harder they try, the worse it gets. Telling people with ADD to try harder only disorganizes them, often to the point where they give up trying. ADD is a neurobiological or "brain" disorder. Current research localizes the problem to the frontal lobes of the brain, the part of the brain that controls concentration, attention span, motivation, judgment, impulse control and organization. When most people with ADD try to concentrate this part of their brain "turns off," rather than "turns on" as it does in most people without ADD.

WINDOWS INTO THE ADD MIND will discuss my experience in diagnosing and treating over 2,500 children, teenagers and adults with ADD. In the book I'll illustrate what ADD "looks like" from the fetus in the mother's womb to childhood, through adolescence and into adult life with real-life stories. I'll explore the potentially serious impact ADD has on relationships, families, school, work and self-esteem. I'll also discuss my work with ADD and a sophisticated brain imaging study called SPECT (single photon emission computed tomography). SPECT has provided valuable insights into the biology of ADD and clues into ADD subtypes. As I'll demonstrate, SPECT has many positive implications for treatment. I'll also discuss how I treat people with ADD at different stages of life. With proper diagnosis and treatment, there is much hope for people with ADD to live happy, productive and fulfilling lives. Without proper diagnosis and treatment, serious problems will probably infect every aspect of the ADD person's life.

This book is not meant to be an exhaustive review of ADD, rather it is a book to help you understand what ADD is, how it can affect a person's day-to-day functioning, what causes it and the major components of effective treatment. By the end of the book, you'll appreciate that ADD is a neurobiological disorder that has serious psychological and social consequences when it goes untreated. Yet, you'll also discover that in the vast majority of cases, ADD is highly treatable, and that treatment can literally change a person's life for the better.

I have not only studied this disorder from a clinical perspective, I have lived it at home. Two of my three children have been diagnosed with ADD (by professionals other than myself). My teenage son has ADD without hyperactivity and my seven-year-old daughter has ADHD (or the hyperactive form). In addition, my wife has been diagnosed with adult ADD. For years, I lived with the guilt that is often associated with having a family member who has this disorder. I thought that I was a terrible husband and a terrible father. These feelings were compounded by the fact that I was a psychiatrist and that I "should" have a perfect marriage and I "should" have well-behaved children. I should know better, I thought. My son use to joke that our family was like the cartoon Simpson family poster that read, "OK, everybody, let's pretend that we're a nice, normal family," as they were getting ready to take a family picture. It was not until my son was first diagnosed, then my daughter, then my wife, that the clouds of guilt began to give way to understanding.

I know this disorder. I know what it is like:

• to chase a child through the store,

• to look on in horror as a four-year-old child darts across a parking lot,

• to watch a child take 4 hours to do 20 minutes of homework,

• to watch a child stare at a writing assignment for hours, unable to get his thoughts from his brain to the paper,

• to have to repeat myself 32 times to get a child up in the morning,

• to be angry every school morning for years because a child is continually 10 minutes late,

• to be amazed that a child's room can become so messy in such a short period of time,

• to always be on the alert in a store or at a friend's house so that my child won't touch or break something,

• to be frustrated by trying to teach a child something, only to have him or her continually distracted by something irrelevant,

♦ to feel guilty about the negative feelings I have toward a child after I've told him not to do something for the umpteenth time,

♦ to be embarrassed to the point of madness in a restaurant (and wonder why I'm spending money to suffer),

♦ to be interrupted without mercy while I'm on the telephone,

♦ to talk with my wife and have her completely miss the meaning of my words, and

♦ to live through angry outbursts with little or no provocation.

I have used the principles in this book to guide the treatment of my patients and to help my own family. I know the information will help you.

Table of Contents

Part I

REAL LIFE STORIES

The following "REAL LIFE STORIES" demonstrate what ADD "looks like" during the life cycle. These stories are all real. The details have been altered to protect the confidentiality of my patients.

CHAPTER 1

Children

================================

Billy, age 9

Billy, age 9, has had trouble in school since starting kindergarten. The teachers seemed to call his parents at least once a month, complaining about Billy's behavior. He interrupted in class, was distractible, had trouble concentrating on his work and was overly active and often out of his seat. The teacher also said that he was impulsive and got into fights with other children, because he "seemed to take things the wrong way." Additionally, Billy's work was sloppy, he often forgot or lost assignments and his desk was so disorganized it was a wonder he could find anything in it at all.

His parents were very confused at what to do. They knew there had been a problem for some time, and they alternated between blaming Billy, blaming the "lousy" school and blaming themselves. When Billy was 5 years old, the mother took him to the pediatrician because of his high activity level and difficult nature. While the mother was talking to the doctor, Billy sat perfectly still and was very polite and attentive to the doctor. The doctor told the mother that there was nothing the matter with Billy and that she should take a parenting classes. The mother left the pediatrician's office in tears because he confirmed her worst fear, which was that she was a defective parent and the cause of Billy's problems. Yet, despite the parenting classes the problems continued.

Homework was always a struggle with Billy. Work that typically took their other kids 30 minutes to complete, took Billy 3 or 4 hours to finish. During his homework, he was up every 5 minutes looking for food or bothering his older sister. He was also a difficult child to parent. He often argued whenever he was told to do something. He said things without thinking and he got emotional with very little provocation. In the first 3 years of school Billy was labeled as a willful, defiant child. He was often sad and frustrated and he had a tendency to blame others for his problems.

In third grade, he was finally brought to see me for an evaluation. It was clear from watching him in my office that he had difficulty concentrating, he was distractible, active and impulsive. Billy had Attention Deficit Disorder.

I placed him on medication, talked with the school on effective classroom management techniques, had his parents attend a special parenting group for dealing with difficult children and taught Billy some specialized biofeedback techniques. Six months after I began seeing Billy he was like a different child. He was less impulsive, his attention span increased and he appeared calmer. His grades also markedly improved. Four years later, he likes himself, he is effective at school and his relationships at home and with friends are "normal."

Shortly after I placed Billy on medication I asked him if he remembered the time in the pediatrician's office when he was five-years-old. Billy nodded that he remembered. I asked him what he was thinking that day and why he was able to sit so still during the interview. He told me that he thought the doctor was going to do brain surgery on him. You could sit still too if you thought someone was going to open up your skull!

Kristie, age 5

Kristie has been affectionately labeled the "pink tornado." Ever since she could walk, she ran. Everywhere. Her parents were always on edge, wondering what she was going to do next. She climbed. Swung on cupboard doors. Ran into the street as soon as her mother's back was turned. And she was her own "little wrecking crew" when she went shopping with her mom or dad. Her parents brought her to see me after she was nearly hit by a car in the parking lot after she opened the car door and ran to the store.

Her mother complained that she could not take Kristie anywhere without a commotion. In restaurants, she wiggled, yelled out, and screamed if she didn't get her way. Other adults would stare at Kristie's parents, with a look that said, "Why don't you beat that bratty child into submission!" Lord knows they spanked this child more than they thought any child should be spanked. That didn't seem to be the answer. In fact, the more they spanked Kristie, the more she would act up. Almost like she was driven for more punishment.

Kristie also had a very short attention span, never played with anything longer than a few minutes and would constantly tear her room apart. Her parents actually put a lock on the outside of her room to keep her out when her parents were not supervising her.

During my first session with Kristie, she tore up my office. She climbed my bookcases. Messed up the papers on my desk. Screamed at her parents when they asked her to settle down. And almost invited her parents to spank her in front of me. Kristie had never been abused and no obvious emotional trauma was evident in her life. The parents, who cared for each other very much, wondered how long they would last as a family.

Clearly, Kristie had a severe case of ADD. It probably had genetic roots. Her mother's father was an alcoholic and her uncle on her father's side was in jail for assault. Kristie also had an aunt who was on Prozac for depression. When I placed Kristie on Ritalin she became more active and aggressive. Dexedrine did the same thing to her. With the atypical response to medication I ordered a brain SPECT study, which showed that she had trouble shifting her attention and she would get stuck on certain thoughts and behavior. With this information, I placed her on Prozac (an antidepressant that also help people with obsessive thoughts) and she calmed down almost immediately. In several weeks she was playful, attentive and much more relaxed. The mother said that it was amazing how much less she was yelling at Kristie. The parents also took a parenting class which helped them learn the necessary skills in dealing with their difficult child.

CHAPTER 2

Teenagers

Louanne, age 16

I met Louanne after her mother had heard me lecture in one of my wife's college classes. When I described ADD, Louanne's mother started to cry, knowing that the symptoms I described fit her daughter. Louanne had a short attention span. She was easily distracted. She often did not finish her assignments. She had a low self-esteem, and she talked incessantly without saying very much of substance.

Louanne had always wanted to be a music teacher, but she began to believe that she couldn't do the work to succeed in college. She felt that she was slow and different from her friends. She was demoralized.

Within a month of starting Louanne on medication, she improved dramatically. I remember her coming into my office so tickled that she could get her work done. Her teachers noticed a marked improvement in her attitude, effort and performance. In the semester after she started treatment, her grades went from a 2.1 to a 3.0. She was especially pleased that she could compete with her friends at school. She did not have to take a back seat to their intellectual superiority over her. Quickly, she developed more hope for herself. Her mother commented that she was more thoughtful when she spoke and that their relationship had also improved. The mother said, "Just knowing that this is a medical disorder, with signs, symptoms and treatment have given us immense hope for Louanne."

Gregg, age 18

When Gregg first came to see me at the age of 14, he was a wreck. He had just been expelled from his third school for fighting and breaking the rules. He told off teachers in the classroom and he picked fights on the school grounds. His parents were at their wits' end and were ready to send him off to a residential treatment center. At home, he was defiant. He didn't do any of his chores. He was restless. He teased his younger brother and sister without mercy. His room was a mess and he challenged his parents about any issue they would bring up. He also never did his homework and he talked about dropping out of school, saying he didn't need an education to take care of himself.

When I first saw him, he was a "turned off" teenager. His eyes looked down and he didn't say much. He told me that he wasn't able to get along with his family, but that he didn't want to be sent away. He also said that school was very hard for him and that he thought he was stupid. When I did a test of verbal intelligence on him, however, his demeanor started to change. He liked the test and seemed challenged by it. His verbal IQ score was 142, in the superior range. I helped him shift his mind set about himself from that of a teenager who was stupid and a troublemaker to one that was very bright but had trouble learning and getting along with others.

Looking back in Gregg's history it was clear he had symptoms of ADD his whole life. He was a fidgety kid. His handwriting was awful. His desk at school was always a mess. He had trouble waiting his turn in school, and the other kids made fun of him, calling him stupid because he had some trouble learning.

Due to the severity of his problems, and the potential departure of Gregg from the family, I ordered a brain SPECT study on Gregg to evaluate the functioning of his brain. The study showed that he had two problems. When Gregg tried to concentrate, the front part of his brain, which should increase in activity, actually decreased in activity. This is the part of the brain which controls attention span, judgment, impulse control and critical thinking. All areas where Gregg was having problems. His brain study also showed that he had decreased activity in his left temporal lobe, which, when abnormal, often causes problems with violence.

As I explained all of this to Gregg, he became visibly relieved. "You mean," he said, "the harder I try to concentrate, the worse it gets for me." "Yes," I replied. He responded very nicely to a combination of medication (Ritalin and Tegretol) to correct the problems in his frontal and temporal lobes. He was able to remain at home, finish high school and start college. When Gregg was properly diagnosed, treated and helped to shift his mind set away from the notion he was a stupid troublemaker, he was able to become a functional member of his family.

CHAPTER 3

Adults

Brett, age 27

Brett, 27, had just been fired from his fourth job in a year. He blamed his boss for expecting too much of him, but it was the same old story. Brett had trouble with details, he was often late to work, he seemed disorganized and he would miss important deadlines. The final straw came when he impulsively told off a difficult customer who complained about his attitude.

Brett's mother was extremely frustrated. All his life Brett had these kind of problems and she was tired of bailing him out. As a teenager he dropped out of school in the eleventh grade, despite being tested as having a high IQ. He was restless and fidgety, very impulsive and his attention span was extremely short. He was also easily distracted and small amounts of homework would take him several hours to complete, even with much nagging and yelling from his mother. He was also a master at getting people angry at him, and it seemed to others that he intentionally stirred things up so that people would become mad.

After Brett's mother read a column that I had written in the local newspaper on adult ADD, she sent him to see me. It was clear from his history that he had a lifelong picture of ADD that had gone unnoticed, even though the mother had Brett tested on three separate occasions. After I placed him on medication and saw him briefly in psychotherapy, his life made a dramatic turn around. He returned to school, finished a technical degree in fire inspection technology and got a job. He has kept that job now for 4 years and feels that he is happier, more focused and more positive than ever before.

Chuck, age 52

Chuck, a college professor, came into therapy because his wife was getting ready to divorce him. She complained that he never talked to her, he was unreliable and he never finished projects that he started. Also, he didn't pay the bills on time, he was tremendously disorganized and he had a very short fuse. As a child, Chuck had the nickname of "Speedy" and, even though he was very smart, he received mediocre to poor grades in school. He said, "They passed me in school to get me out of their hair." Chuck had many different teaching jobs and was bored easily.

After the marital therapist did an evaluation on the couple, she referred Chuck to me, believing he might have ADD. She was right. After I placed Chuck on medication he, and his wife, reported that he was calmer and more focused. He was a better listener and was much more organized. Several months after he started on the medication, school let out and he forgot to take his medication. Within several days, his wife noticed the difference and was upset with him. She told him, "Why do we have to live with this chaos? Take your medication!" When he went back on his medication things were much improved and remain so. The marriage counseling went quickly and was very effective for this couple.

Lindy, age 37

Lindy was ready to leave her husband when she first came to see me. "We fight all the time," she said. "Not over big things...but it sure gets old." Lindy also complained that she was moody, often irritable and that she yelled at her children a lot. "I know it's not good for them! I just seem not to be able to help it," she said tearfully. She had taken a parenting class several years before, but she had trouble following through with the recommendations the instructor gave her. She also had trouble getting to sleep and it was a real struggle for her to get out of bed in the morning.

When I first saw Lindy, she was in the process of going back to college. When she first went to college at age 18, she got mostly Cs and Ds. "I had a lot of trouble getting my term papers in on time," she complained. Since she has gone back to college, her motivation to succeed is much higher, but she complains that it is hard to remain focused in class, she is easily distracted, and keeping up with taking notes is almost impossible for her.

Lindy's husband complained that she was hard to live with. She was irritable, she seemed to provoke fights with him or the children, and she had to have things a certain way or she'd become very upset. "Everyone takes off their shoes and socks before they come into the house. And if she sees a strand of hair, she becomes very upset! She's the only person I've ever met who vacuums the house at 11P.M. on Friday night." He said that there were sexual problems. When they were making love, she'd often become distracted and lose interest. She'd then be in the mood to just get it over with. The husband often felt that she was having an affair.

Lindy's grandfather, father and brother had problems with alcohol. She also had a niece and a nephew who responded very well to Ritalin. As I listened to her story, along with the comments from her husband, it was clear that Lindy had the "overfocusing" subtype of ADD, where she had trouble shifting her attention from thing to thing. This caused her to have to have things a certain way at home and made it hard for her to take notes in school. She responded nicely to a combination of Ritalin and Prozac. After several months, she was more relaxed at home, school was much easier for her, she was better with the children and her relationship with her husband was more positive.

CHAPTER 4

Families

Tim, Pam, Paul and Karen

Paul, age 20, first came to see me because he was having trouble finishing his senior year at a Northern California university. He was having trouble completing term papers, he could not focus in class and he had little motivation. He began to believe that he should drop out of school and go to work for his father. He hated the idea of quitting school so close to graduation. He came to see me on a referral from a friend who had a younger brother whom I had helped. In his history, Paul also told me about bouts of depression, that he had and he had even been treated with Prozac in the past with little benefit. Paul's brain SPECT study was consistent with both depression and ADD. He had a wonderful response to a combination of an antidepressant and stimulant medication. He finished college and got the kind of job he wanted.

When Paul's mother, Pam, saw what a nice response he had to treatment, she came to see me for herself. As a child, she had trouble learning. Even though she was very artistic, she had little motivation for school and her teachers labeled her as an underachiever. As an adult, Pam went back to school and earned her degree in elementary school teaching. In order to student teach, however, she had to pass the National Teacher's Exam. She had failed the test on four occasions. Pam was ready to give up and try a new avenue of study when she saw Paul get better. She thought maybe there was help for her. In fact, she had a brain study very similar to Paul's study and she responded to the same combination of medication. Four months later she passed the National Teacher's Exam.

With two successes in the family, the mother then sent her 19-year-old daughter, Karen, to see me. Like her brother, Karen was a bright child who had underachieved in school. At the time she came to see me, she lived in Los Angeles and she was enrolled in a broadcast journalism course. She complained that learning the material was hard for her. She was also moody, restless, easily distracted, impulsive and had a quick temper. Several years earlier she was treated for alcohol abuse and using amphetamines. She said that the alcohol settled her restlessness and the amphetamines helped her to concentrate. Karen's brain SPECT study was very similar to her brother's and mother's. Once on medication, she was amazed at the difference. She could concentrate in class and she finished her work in half the time as before. Karen's level of confidence increased to the point where she could go and look for work as a broadcaster, something she had been unable to do previously.

The most reluctant member of the family to see me was the father, Tim. Even though Pam, Paul and Karen told him that he should see me, he balked at the idea. He said, "There's nothing wrong with me; look at how successful I am." But his family knew different. Even though Tim owned a successful grocery store, he was reclusive and distant. He got tired early in the day, he was easily distracted and he was scattered in his approach to work. He was successful at work, in part, because he had very good people who took his ideas and made them happen. He also had trouble learning new games, such as cards. This caused him to avoid many social situations. Tim enjoyed high stimulation activities and he loved riding motorcycles, even at the age of 55. Looking back, Tim had done poorly in high school. He barely passed college even though he had a very high IQ. He tended to drift from job to job until he was able to buy the grocery store from a widow whose husband had recently died. Tim's wife finally convinced him to see me. She was getting ready to divorce him, because he would never talk with her in the evening. She felt that he didn't care about her. He later told me that he was physically and emotionally drained.

During my first session with Tim he told me that he couldn't possibly have ADD because he was a success in business. But the more questions I asked him about his past, the more lights went on his head. At the end of the interview my comment back to him was that, "If you really do have ADD, I wonder how successful you could be given what you've already accomplished." Tim's brain study showed the classic pattern for ADD. When he tried to concentrate the frontal lobes of his brain turned off, rather than on. When I told him this, it really sunk in. "Maybe that is why it is hard for me to learn games. When I'm in a social situation and I'm pressed to learn or respond, I just freeze up. So I avoid these situations."

Tim had a remarkable response to Ritalin. He was more awake during the day, he accomplished more in less time and his relationship with his wife dramatically improved. In fact, they both said they couldn't believe that their relationship could be so good, after all the years of distance and hurt.

Phillip and Dennis

Nine-year-old Phillip was frightened when the police came to his school to talk to him. His teacher had noticed bruises on his legs and arms and she called Child Protective Services. He wasn't sure if he should tell them that his father, Dennis, had beaten him up, or if he should say that he fell down a flight of stairs or something like that. Phillip did not want to get his dad into trouble and he felt responsible for the beating he received. After all, he reasoned, his father had told him ten times to clean his room and for some reason, unknown to Phillip, he hadn't done it. Phillip and his father often fought, but it had never been apparent to people outside the home. Phillip decided to tell the truth, hoping that it would help his family get some help.

Indeed, Phillip's family did get help. The court ordered the father to undergo a psychiatric evaluation and counseling for the family. The father was found to have a short fuse and he was impulsive and explosive in many different situations. He began to have problems with aggressiveness after he sustained a head injury in a car accident six years ago. His wife reported that when Phillip was first born, the father was loving, patient and attentive. After the accident, he was irritable, distant and angry.

In family counseling sessions I noticed that Phillip was a very difficult child. He was restless, active, impulsive and defiant. When his parents told him to stop doing annoying behaviors, he just ignored them and continued irritating those around him. I soon discovered it was the interaction between Phillip and his father that was the problem and counseling alone would not be helpful. I believed there was some underlying biological or physical "brain problem" that contributed to the abusive interactions. In an effort to further understand the biology of this family's problems, I ordered brain SPECT studies on both Phillip and Dennis.

The brain SPECT studies for both Phillip and his father were abnormal. The father's study clearly showed an area of increased activity in his left temporal lobe (near the temples), probably a result from the car accident. Several researchers have demonstrated left temporal lobe problems to be associated with people who have a short fuse and a tendency toward violence. Phillip's SPECT study revealed decreased activity in the front part of his brain when he tried to concentrate. This finding is often found in kids who are impulsive and overly active.

After taking a history, watching the family interact and reviewing the SPECT studies, it was clear to me that Phillip's and his father's problems were, in part, biological. I placed both of them on medication. The father was put on an anti-seizure medication to calm his left temporal lobe, and Phillip was placed on a stimulant medication to increase activity in the front part of his brain.

Once the underlying biological problems were treated, the family was then able to benefit from psychotherapy and begin to heal the wounds of abuse. In counseling sessions Phillip was calmer and more attentive and the father was more able to constructively learn how to deal with Phillip's difficult behavior.

Whenever child abuse occurs it is a severe tragedy. It may become an even a worse tragedy, however, if people ignore the underlying brain problems that may be contributing to the problems. In this case and in many others, it is often the interaction between a difficult child and an aggressive, impulsive parent that leads to the problem. These negative interactions may have a biological basis to them. To be effective in helping these families, it is very important to understand the underlying biological or "brain" contribution to the problem.

CHAPTER 5

Abraham Lincoln's Son Tad and a Brief History of ADD

The syndrome that is now called ADD was first described in mid 1800s after a child experienced a head injury or brain infection. The syndrome included problems with attention span, hyperactivity, and impulsivity.

It is likely that Abraham Lincoln's third son, Tad, had ADD. He was described as an impulsive, uninhibited child who would throw monumental temper tantrums when he failed to get his way. In the White House, Tad would run and shout through the corridors, break into cabinet meetings and chase his brother around visiting politicians. At times, Tad would go through the White House ringing bells and setting off alarms. Some described him as nervous, like his mother. Others said he was a hyperactive child with a speech impediment who was slow to learn. His mother hired many tutors for him, who one after another quit in frustration over his unteachability.

ADD is not a new disorder!

In the 1940s, the idea of "minimal brain damage" was postulated because no one could see anything physically different from "normal" brains.

In the 1950s, the idea of a brain filtering defect was discussed, whereby the child was overstimulated and unable to control his behavior.

In the 1960s, the idea of minimal brain dysfunction was popular. Physicians believed that it was biological, but again had no way to prove it.

In 1975, the first evidence for the brain being understimulated was introduced with the use of more advanced electroencephalograms (EEG or brainwave studies). This began to make the most sense, because hyperactive children often responded nicely to stimulant medications.

In 1990, Alan Zametkin, M.D. at the National Institutes of Mental Health published brain imaging data that supported the notion of brain under-activity, especially in response to an intellectual challenge. The more the person with ADD tries to concentrate, the harder it becomes.

VARIOUS NAMES FOR THE DISORDER

ADD has had many names through the years. Here is a small sample:

Hyperkinesis (excessive movement)

Minimal Brain Dysfunction

Hyperactive Child Syndrome

Hyperkinetic Reaction of Childhood (DSM-II)

Attention Deficit Disorder, With or Without Hyperactivity (DSM-III)

Attention Deficit Hyperactivity Disorder (DSM-IIIR)

Undifferentiated Attention Deficit Disorder (DSM-IIIR)

Attention Deficit/Hyperactivity Disorder (DSM-IV)

** spulkis (Yiddish for "ants in the pants")

Note: DSM stands for the Diagnostic and Statistical Manual of the American Psychiatric Association which is used as a diagnostic reference for clinicians all over the world. It is continually updated to reflect the clinical and research trends of psychiatric medicine.

HOW COMMON IS ADD?

ADD is the most common psychiatric problem in children, affecting approximately 50% of children and teens who come to mental health clinics for evaluation.

** It is estimated that 5 - 10% of the childhood population has ADD.

** The male/female Ratio of ADD varies anywhere from 2:1 to 10:1, depending on the study you read. Most studies report a ratio of about 6:1.

Clinically, I think that ADD is markedly underdiagnosed in girls. Here are some of the reasons:

  -- girls often do not have the hyperactive component;

  -- they do not have as much testosterone and are less aggressive;

  -- they are less disruptive;

  -- there are different societal expectations for girls, so that if they do not achieve, they are labeled as slow or uninterested and not pushed as much as boys to reach their potential.

ADD is the most commonly diagnosed psychiatric disorder in children. It is therefore surprising that many pediatricians and teachers are not more aware of it.

PART II

WHAT IS ADD?

How Do I Know If I Have It?

CHAPTER 6

What Is ADD?

Attention Deficit Disorder (ADD) is a neurobiological syndrome which affect many aspects of a person's life. Attention span difficulties, distractibility, impulsivity and restlessness are the cornerstone symptoms of this disorder. ADD used to be thought of as a disorder of hyperactive, male children, who outgrew it as they became teenagers. What we now know, is that **ADD affects millions of girls and women**, and that **most people do not outgrow it**. Most people diagnosed with ADD as children continue with symptoms into adulthood. It is estimated that ADD affects approximately 17 million people in the US.

In my experience, there are five major subtypes of ADD, along with various combinations:

ADD, with hyperactivity (classic AD/HD)
ADD, without hyperactivity (couch potatoes)
ADD, overfocused (tend to get stuck)
ADD, depressive (negative and irritable)
ADD, violent, explosive (dark thoughts)

Here are the major symptoms for the subtypes. I have included the part of the brain suspected to be involved with each subtype in parentheses.

CRITERIA FOR AD/HD
Attention-Deficit/Hyperactivity
Disorder from DSM-IV
(Prefrontal Cortex System)

Either (1) or (2)

(1) six (or more) of the following symptoms of inattention have persisted for at least six months to a degree that is maladaptive and inconsistent with developmental level:

Inattention

_____ 1. often fails to give close attention to details or makes careless mistakes in schoolwork, work, or other activities
_____ 2. often has difficulty sustaining attention in tasks or play activities
_____ 3. often does not seem to listen when spoken to directly
_____ 4. often does not follow through on instructions and fails to finish schoolwork, chores, or duties in the workplace (not due to oppositional behavior or failure to understand instructions)
_____ 5. often has difficulty organizing tasks and activities
_____ 6. often avoids, dislikes, or is reluctant to engage in tasks that require sustained mental effort (such as schoolwork or homework)
_____ 7. often loses things necessary for tasks or activities (e.g., toys, school assignments, pencils, books, or tools)
_____ 8. is often easily distracted by extraneous stimuli
_____ 9. is often forgetful in daily activities

(2) six (or more) of the following symptoms of **hyperactivity-impulsivity** have persisted for at least six months to a degree that is maladaptive and inconsistent with developmental level:

Hyperactivity

_____ 1. often fidgets with hands or feet or squirms in seat
_____ 2. often leaves seat in classroom or in other situations in which remaining seated is expected

___ 3. often runs about or climbs excessively in situations in which it is inappropriate (in adolescents or adults, may be limited to subjective feelings of restlessness)

___ 4. often has difficulty playing or engaging in leisure activities quietly

___ 5. is often "on the go" or often acts as if "driven by a motor"

___ 6. often talks excessively

Impulsivity

___ 7. often blurts out answers before questions have been completed

___ 8. often has difficulty awaiting turn

___ 9. often interrupts or intrudes on others (e.g., butts into conversations or games)

The onset of at least some symptoms must be before age seven and they must have lasted at least for six months. In order to make the diagnosis, some impairment from the symptoms is present in two or more settings (e.g., school [or work] and at home). There must also be clear evidence of clinically significant impairment in social, academic, or occupational functioning. The severity of the disorder is rated as mild, moderate or severe.

Based on DSM-IV criteria, there can be three subtypes:

AD/HD, combined type,
    if both criterion for 1 and 2 are met

AD/HD, predominantly inattentive type,
    if criterion 1 is met but criterion 2 is not

AD/HD, predominantly hyperactive-impulsive type,
    if criterion 2 is met but criterion 1 is not

The boys with AD/HD combined or predominantly hyperactive-impulsive type are often identified early in life. The level of hyperactivity, restlessness and impulsivity causes them to stand out from others. AD/HD predominantly inattentive type girls, on the other hand, may be ignored because they get labeled as "social butterflies." Even as we near the 21rst century, societal expectations are different for girls than for boys.

Brain studies of patients with classic AD/HD reveal a decrease in brain activity in the frontal lobes of the brain in response to an intellectual challenge. The harder these people try to concentrate, the worse it gets.

Classic ADHD is usually very responsive to stimulant medications, such as Ritalin, Dexedrine, Cylert, Desoxyn, and Adderal. These medications "turn on" the frontal lobes and prevent the shutdown which often occurs with ADD.

Additional Symptoms Notes For ADHD:

1. Restless, fidgety
-- like a mosquito buzzing around the environment, or
-- a bullet ricocheting off the walls,
-- jitterbug, others note excessive movement
-- legs or fingers in constant motion
-- hyperactivity

2. Problems remaining seated
-- up, down, all around
-- swinging around in seat
-- constantly up

3. Easily distracted by extraneous stimuli
-- trouble remaining focused
-- hears whatever else is going on
-- if someone drops a pencil three rows over, their attention immediately
   goes to the pencil and distracts them from their task

4. Problems taking turns
-- need to have way immediately
-- often tries to cut to the front of the line
-- alienates themselves socially from others

5. Responds impulsively or without thinking
-- most people have a little brake in their brain that causes them to think; before they act, people with ADD seem to be missing that brake and react often without forethought

6. Problems completing things
-- homework, school work, chores
-- start many things that they do not finish

7. Difficulty with sustained attention or erratic attention
-- short attention span for most things
-- people with ADD may be able to concentrate on things that are new (sitting in the pediatrician's office), novel, highly interesting (video games) or frightening (dad coming home from work after mom has called him out of a meeting)

8. Shifts from one uncompleted activity to another
-- with a short attention span, the ADD person often will go from activity to activity, toy to toy or project to project

9. Difficulty playing quietly
-- often described as noisy, loud, or intrusive (this may be very difficult for a mother who is sensitive to noise)

10. Talks excessively
-- phrases such as "motor mouth," or "who put a quarter in you" are often heard with these people

11. Interrupts frequently
-- blurts out answers in class even after being warned time after time. Often this is upsetting and embarrassing for parents

12. Doesn't seem to listen
-- this may seem somewhat selective, people with ADD often absorb less than 30% of what is said, causing misperception and misinterpretation

13. Disorganization
-- book bag,
-- homework,
-- room,
-- desk,
-- office,
-- paperwork
-- time (often late or in a hurry)
-- overall organization is a problem

14. Takes high risks
-- these children are at risk for accidents (running into the street without thinking, getting hold of medication that is left out, climbing up cupboards or on top of appliances, etc.)

Additional Symptoms

-- often poor handwriting; as adults, they may print
-- trouble writing, even though they may be able to say what they are thinking. They have trouble writing what they are thinking (this has been termed finger agnosia)
-- often have difficulty getting to sleep and have trouble getting up in the morning
-- cannot tune out the edges and concentrate on the middle
-- poor memory, scattered
-- poor follow through
-- homework takes forever
-- they tend to be very stimulation-seeking and are experts at getting others angry at them
-- easily frustrated
-- poor eye tracking
-- poor self-esteem, especially with late diagnosis
-- chronic failure to master social and academic situations
-- unpleasant reaction from others due to their behavior
-- suffer from an overdose of criticism
-- children are often demoralized and may look depressed
-- decreased coordination compared to peers
-- many have "soft neurological signs" such as fine motor problems

HALLMARKS OF ADD without Hyperactivity
(these are often helpful indicators I've found for
AD/HD, Predominantly Inattentive Type)
(Also Prefrontal Cortex System)

Six or more of the following symptoms are indicative of ADD without hyperactivity.

____ 1. Difficulty with sustained attention or erratic attention span
____ 2. Easily distracted by extraneous stimuli
____ 3. Excessive daydreaming
____ 4. Disorganized
____ 5. Responds impulsively or without thinking
____ 6. Problems completing things
____ 7. Doesn't seem to listen
____ 8. Shifts from one uncompleted activity to another
____ 9. Often complains of being bored
____10. Often appears to be apathetic or unmotivated
____11. Frequently sluggish or slow moving
____12. Frequently spacy or internally preoccupied

The onset of these symptoms often becomes apparent later in childhood or even adolescence. The brighter the individual, the later symptoms seem to become a problem. The symptoms must be present for at least six months and not be related to a depressive episode. The severity of the disorder is rated as mild, moderate or severe.

Even though these children have many of the same symptoms of the people with AD/HD, they are not hyperactive and may, in fact, be hypoactive. Girls are frequently missed because they are more likely to have this type of ADD. In addition, they may: daydream excessively, complain of being bored, appear apathetic or unmotivated, appear frequently sluggish or slow moving or appear spacy or internally preoccupied -- the classic "couch potato." Most people with this form of ADD are never diagnosed. They do not exhibit enough symptoms that "grate" on the environment to cause people to seek help for them. Yet, they often experience severe disability from the disorder. Instead of help, they get labeled as willful, uninterested, or defiant.

As with the AD/HD subtype, brain studies in patients with ADD, inattentive subtype reveal a decrease in brain activity in the frontal lobes of the brain in response to an intellectual challenge. Again, it seems that the harder these people try to concentrate, the worse it gets. ADD, inattentive subtype is often very responsive to stimulant medications listed above, at a percentage somewhat less than the AD/HD patients.

HALLMARKS OF ADD
Overfocused Subtype
(Cingulate System)

Six or more of the following symptoms are indicative of ADD overfocused (1 and 2 are needed to make the diagnosis).

____ 1. Difficulty with sustained attention or erratic attention span
____ 2. Easily distracted by extraneous stimuli
____ 3. Excessive or senseless worrying
____ 4. Disorganized or superorganized
____ 5. Oppositional, argumentative
____ 6. Strong tendency to get locked into negative thoughts, having the same thought over and over
____ 7. Tendency toward compulsive behavior
____ 8. Intense dislike for change
____ 9. Tendency to hold grudges
____10. Trouble shifting attention from subject to subject
____11. Difficulties seeing options in situations
____12. Tendency to hold on to own opinion and not listen to others
____13. Tendency to get locked into a course of action, whether or not it is good for the person
____14. Needing to have things done a certain way or becomes very upset
____15. Others complain that you worry too much
____16. A strong tendency to hold grudges, to hold on to hurts from the past.

People with ADD, overfocused subtype, tend to get locked into things and they have trouble shifting their attention from thought to thought. This subtype has a very specific brain pattern, showing increased blood flow in the top, middle portion of the frontal lobes. This is the part of the brain that allows you to shift your attention from thing to thing. When this part of the brain is working too hard, people have trouble shifting their attention and end up "stuck" on thoughts or behaviors.

This brain pattern may present itself differently among family members. For example, a mother or father with ADD overfocused subtype may experience trouble focusing along with obsessive thoughts (repetitive negative thoughts) or have compulsive behaviors (hand washing, checking, counting, etc.), the son or daughter may be oppositional (get stuck on saying no, no way, never, you can't make me do it), and another family member may find change very hard for them.

This pattern is often very responsive to new "anti-obsessive antidepressants," which increase the neurotransmitter serotonin in the brain. I have nicknamed these medications as my "anti-stuck medications." These medications include Prozac, Paxil, Zoloft, Anafranil, and Effexor.

HALLMARKS OF ADD
Depressive Subtype
(Limbic System)

Six or more of the following symptoms are indicative of ADD depressive subtype (1 and 2 are needed to make the diagnosis).

___ 1. Difficulty with sustained attention or erratic attention span
___ 2. Easily distracted by extraneous stimuli
___ 3. Moodiness
___ 4. Negativity
___ 5. Low energy
___ 6. Irritability
___ 7. Social isolation
___ 8. Hopelessness, helplessness, excessive guilt
___ 9. Disorganization
___10. Lowered sexual interest
___11. Sleep changes (too much or too little)
___12. Forgetfulness
___13. Low self-esteem

It is very important to differentiate this subtype of ADD from clinical depression. This is best done by evaluating the symptoms over time. ADD, depressive subtype, is consistent over time and there must have been evidence from childhood and adolescence. It does not just show up at the age of 35 when someone is going through serious stress in their life. It must be a pattern of behavior over time. Major depressive disorders tend to cycle. There are periods of normalcy which alternate with periods of depression.

The medications used for ADD, depressive subtype include standard antidepressants, such as Tofranil (imipramine), Norpramin (desipramine), and Pamelor (nortryptiline), the newer antidepressants such as Prozac and Wellbutrin (buprion), and the stimulants. Clinically, I have been very impressed with the ability of stimulants to help this subtype of ADD. This is why it is very important to differentiate this subtype from primary depressive disorders.

HALLMARKS OF ADD
Explosive Subtype
(Temporal Lobe Subtype)

Six or more of the following symptoms are indicative of ADD violent, explosive (1 and 2 are needed to make the diagnosis).

____ 1. Difficulty with sustained attention or erratic attention span
____ 2. Easily distracted by extraneous stimuli
____ 3. Impulse control problems
____ 4. Short fuse or periods of extreme irritability
____ 5. Periods of rages with little provocation
____ 6. Often misinterprets comments as negative when they are not
____ 7. Irritability builds, then explodes, then recedes; often tired after a rage
____ 8. Periods of spaciness or confusion
____ 9. Periods of panic or fear for no specific reason
____10. Visual changes, such as seeing shadows or objects changing shape
____11. Frequent periods of deja vu (feelings of being somewhere before even though you never have)
____12. Sensitivity or mild paranoia
____13. History of a head injury or family history of violence or explosiveness
____14. Dark thoughts; may involve suicidal or homicidal thoughts
____15. Periods of forgetfulness or memory problems

In my clinical experience, temporal lobe symptoms are found in approximately 10-15% of patients with ADD. Temporal lobe symptoms can be among the most painful. These include periods of panic or fear for no specific reason, periods of spaciness or confusion, dark thoughts (such as suicidal or homicidal thoughts), significant social withdrawal, frequent periods of deja vu, irritability, rages, and visual changes (such as things getting bigger or smaller than they really are). Temporal lobe dysfunction may be inherited or it may be caused by some sort of brain trauma.

Temporal lobe symptoms associated with ADD are often very responsive to anti-seizure medication, such as Tegretol or Depakote.

SYMPTOMS MAY CHANGE
ACCORDING TO THE SITUATION

The variability of ADD symptoms often confuses doctors and may lead to late diagnosis or misdiagnosis.

** The degree of structure matters. The higher degree of structure in the environment causes these children to be distinguishable from non-ADD children.

** These children are often more compliant and less disruptive with their fathers (dads are firmer, use less words and generally spend less time with the kids so they are less worn down than the mothers).

** These children are more "on task" when the instructions are repeated frequently.

** These children display fewer behavior problems in new, novel, highly stimulating or frightening situations (such as in medical or psychiatric evaluations, playing video games or watching TV).

CHAPTER 7

Other Things To Look For In Diagnosing ADD

When ADD is present, these other problems should also be evaluated. Sometimes these problems are misdiagnosed as ADD, sometimes they are co-morbid or run together with ADD. After reading this chapter you'll begin to understand the complexity of the disorder. This is one of the reasons it is important to have a thorough evaluation by a competent professional who understands ADD.

Emotional/Adjustment Problems

Emotional and adjustment problems can masquerade as ADD, be a result of ADD, or occur together with ADD. Here is a sample of the problems:

** Adjustment Disorders or Family Problems: Temporarily, family problems or significant stress can cause a person of any age to have problems with concentration or restlessness. The difference between stress and ADD is history and duration of the difficulties. ADD is a long-standing problem, which is relatively constant over time. Long-term family problems can cause a child to look as though he or she has ADD from the stress. It must be determined, however, whether or not the serious family problems are a result of ADD in one or more of the family members.

** Behavioral Problems not related to ADD: Some behavior problems have nothing to do with ADD. When parents have ineffective parenting skills, they can actually encourage difficult behavior in their children.

** Depressive Disorders: Depression may be confused with ADD, especially in children. Depressive symptoms include poor memory, low energy, negativity, periods of helplessness and hopelessness, social isolation, along with sleep and appetite changes. Many of these symptoms are also found in ADD. History is the key to proper diagnosis. ADD symptoms are generally constant over time. Depression tends to fluctuate. Many people with ADD experience demoralization (from chronic failure) and may indeed look depressed when ADD is the primary problem. Depression and ADD might also occur concurrently.

** Manic-Depressive Disorder: Manic-Depressive or Bipolar symptoms may be similar to ADD. Both experience restless, excessive talking, hyperactivity, racing thoughts, and impulsivity. The difference is usually found in severity, consistency, and course of the symptoms. ADD remains constant, Bipolar Disorder fluctuates from highs to lows. People who have ADD are usually distractible, restless, and impulsive. People with Bipolar Disorder will have periods of distractibility, restlessness, and impulsivity, but these often fluctuate with depressive episodes and periods of relative calm or normalcy. The manic highs with Bipolar Disorder are not experienced by people with ADD. These highs may reach psychotic proportions and include delusions and/or hallucinations. I have seen these two disorders run together in the same person and I often see them in the same family. In fact, Tad Lincoln, whom I discussed earlier as possibly having ADD, had two parents who experienced severe depression (both President Lincoln and Mary Todd Lincoln had serious depressive episodes, and Mrs. Lincoln probably had a Bipolar Disorder. She experienced severe anger outbursts, pathological jealousy, and periods of psychosis.)

** Anxiety Disorders: Anxiety disorders can present symptoms similar to ADD, such as restlessness, hyperactivity, forgetfulness, and an inability to concentrate. Again, the key to proper diagnosis is history. Anxiety disorders tend to fluctuate; ADD symptoms are generally constant. Having ADD can breed symptoms of anxiety or nervousness. For example, when your mind turns off when it is presented with stress can cause nervousness in social situations or cause fear when you have to speak in front of a group of others.. It is common for people with ADD to experience significant anxiety from underachievement. These disorders also commonly run together.

** Obsessive Compulsive Disorder (OCD): OCD is marked by a person who has obsessions (repetitive negative thoughts) and/or compulsions (repetitive negative behaviors), which interfere with their lives. People with OCD get "stuck" or "locked in" to negative thoughts or behaviors. In my clinical experience there is a high percentage of people with ADD who also have features of

OCD, especially if there is significant alcohol abuse in their family background. The overfocused subtype of ADD has many features in common with OCD, and both disorders tend to respond best to anti-obsessive antidepressants, such as Prozac, Paxil, Anafranil or Zoloft.

** Tic Disorders, such as Gilles de la Tourette's Disorder: Tic disorders are more common among people with ADD. Tics are abnormal, involuntary motor movements, such as blinking, shoulder shrugging, head jerking, or vocal sounds, such as throat clearing, coughing, blowing and even swearing. Gilles de la Tourette's Disorder occurs when there are both motor and vocal tics that have been present for more than a year. Up to 60% of people who have Tourette's also have ADD, and 40-50% of people with Tourette's have OCD. Many clinicians believe that there is a significant connection between ADD, OCD and Tourette's.

** History of physical, emotional or sexual abuse: Abuse of any form can cause learning and behavior problems. Certainly, they can also occur together. Many clinicians see an increased incidence of abuse occurring in families with ADD. The increased level of frustration, impulse control problems and anger found in ADD families causes these families to be more at risk. An accurate, detailed history is necessary to distinguish between abuse and ADD. People who have been abused present more clearly with symptoms of Post Traumatic Stress Disorder (PTSD), such as nightmares, fearfulness, quick startle, flashbacks, feeling numb or emotionally restricted. Yet, many people who have ADD feel they have a form of PTSD from the chronic dysfunction they have experienced.

Learning/Developmental Problems

Learning problems, other than ADD, occur in approximately 40% of people with ADD. Suspect the diagnosis of a learning problem whenever there is long-standing underachievement in school or work. Learning disorders are evaluated by medical evaluation, history, family and school history, and clinical observation The diagnosis is confirmed by "psycho-educational" testing.

Psycho-educational testing evaluates 3 areas:

1) IQ and cognitive style (look for discrepancies between verbal and performance scores,)

2) level of academic skill (standard achievement tests)

3) evidence of a specific learning disabilities or problems (Woodcock-Johnson Psycho-educational Battery)

Computer Model Of Learning Disabilities

Input -- Integration -- Memory -- Output

Input

Visual perception problems: difficulty organizing the position and shape of what they see.

reversed letters or numbers (normal to age 6),

problems focusing on primary figures; may be confused in large, open spaces (malls),

problems judging distances (walking into walls, falling off chairs, knock over a drink),

problems with sports (catching, throwing, hitting).

Auditory perception difficulties: difficulty accurately hearing and organizing sounds.

problems distinguishing subtle sounds, blue/blow, can/can't, ball/bell,

problems focusing on primary sounds,

auditory lag (process sounds more slowly than others),

may misunderstand what is said, appear spacy or internally preoccupied.

Sensory integrative disorder: tactile, proprioceptive, and vestibular inputs.

tactile, confuse input from light touch versus deep touch (pressure),

can be tactilely defensive, sensitive to touch, not like being held, tags, socks may be uncomfortable,

proprioception, confused with body in space, fine and gross motor coordination problems,

vestibular, problems with body movement, may enjoy rocking, spinning in chairs, on swings to settle them,

Taste/Smell: supersensitive to tastes or smells, may make them picky eaters.

Integration: may be auditory or visual

Sequencing: letter order, word order, fact order, sound order (problems dressing or cooking in right sequence, problems following directions).

Abstraction: meaning inferred from sequence, trouble understanding jokes, puns, idioms,

give literal meaning to words, appear mildly paranoid.

Organizing: notes, lockers, book bags, rooms, assignments, difficulty organizing time, often late.

Memory, may be auditory or visual

Short-term memory, remembering up to several minutes, may have to repeat things over and over and over (more common), forgetting what was read, forgetting studies spelling words, forgetting concepts.

Long-term memory, more permanent storage.

Output (expression)

Language

> language production (asked questions by others) may be hard (uses monosyllabic words such as fine, OK, huh?, what?) problems with small talk, often shy in social situations,

> while spontaneous language is often easy.

Motor: coordinating muscles

> gross motor, clumsiness,

> fine motor, poor writing skills.

Examples of Specific Disorders

Academic Skills Disorders
Developmental Reading
Developmental Writing
Developmental Math

Language and Speech Disorders
Developmental Articulation
Developmental Expressive Language
Developmental Receptive Language

Motor Skills Disorder
Developmental Coordination Disorder

Questions To Ask In Evaluating Learning Disorders

Reading

How well do you read?

Do you like to read?

When you read, do you make mistakes like skipping words or lines or reading the same line twice?

Do you find that you don't remember what you read, even though you've read all the words?

Writing

How's your handwriting?

Spelling, grammar, punctuation?

Do you have trouble copying off the board?

Do you usually write in cursive or print?

Do you have trouble getting thoughts from your brain to the paper?

Math

Do you know your multiplication tables?

Do you switch numbers around?

Do you sometimes forget what you're supposed to be doing in the middle of a problem?

Sequencing

When you speak do you have trouble getting everything in the right order (switch words or ideas around)?

Tell me the months of the year.

Do you have trouble using the alphabet in order?

Do you have to start from the beginning each time?

Abstraction

Do you understand jokes when your friends tell them?

Do you sometimes get confused when people seem to say something, yet they tell you they meant something else?

Organization

What does your notebook (room, desk, locker, book bag) look like?

Are your papers organized or a mess?

Do you have multiple piles everywhere?

Do you have trouble organizing your thoughts or the facts you're learning into a whole concept?

Do you have trouble planning your time?

Memory

Do you find that you can learn something at night and then go to school the next day and forget what you have learned?

Do you sometimes forget what you're going to say right in the middle of saying it?

Language

When someone is speaking, do you often have trouble keeping up or understanding what is being said?

Do you often misunderstand people and give the wrong answer?

Do you have problems finding the right words to use?

Treatment

The specific treatments for learning disabilities are beyond the scope of the book. When they occur, it is important for the school system to assist with an assessment for special services or special education to evaluate the need for alternative learning strategies and academic accommodations.

Medical Factors

The following medical factors also need to be considered in fully evaluating ADD:

** Gestational problems, such as maternal alcohol or drug use during pregnancy

** Birth traumas, such as oxygen deprivation or injury

** History of head trauma

** Seizure disorders

** Physical illness/disease, such as thyroid disease or lead exposure

** Severe allergies to environmental toxins or food

** Medications, such as asthma medications.

As you can see from this chapter, evaluating ADD is a complicated process and cannot be done with simple checklists. Get an expert to evaluate you.

CHAPTER 8

ADD Through The Lifecycle

Here's a look at ADD throughout the life cycle. It is important to note that ADD does not just appear in the teenage years or in adulthood. When you know what to look for, ADD symptoms have been present for most of a person's life.

-- Many children are noted to be overly active in the womb (one mother once told me that her unborn child broke her 9th rib by kicking her during the eighth month of pregnancy).

-- Many are difficult from birth, colicky, fussy eaters, have a difficult time being comforted, are sensitive to noise and touch, and have eating and sleeping difficulties.

-- As toddlers, they're often excessively active, mischievous, demanding, difficult to toilet train and noncompliant with parental requests (like the terrible twos that are continued...)

-- Most are first recognized in kindergarten, first or second grade; school teachers often notice the difference between these children and normal children, because they have a large database of normal behavior.

-- For hyperactive boys, by the time they have entered school, problems with aggression, defiance and oppositional behavior have often emerged. These problems often lead to social isolation and poor self-esteem.

-- The majority of ADD kids have varying degrees of poor school performance related to failure to finish assigned tasks, disruptive behavior during class, poor peer relations. The time that these problems become apparent often relates to intelligence and the school setting. Often the brighter the child, the later he or she is diagnosed. Up until that time, the child is likely to be labeled as an underachiever, willful, defiant or oppositional.

-- Approximately 40% have significant learning disabilities in addition to ADD, especially in the area of reading, spelling, handwriting, math or language.

-- As teenagers, approximately 25% fully outgrow their symptoms. However, most do not outgrow their symptoms at puberty as previously thought and they have difficulty with their family, school or the community!! The error occurred in part because most ADD children outgrow the hyperactive component before or at puberty. Unfortunately, problems with inattentiveness and impulsivity remain and tens of thousands of teenagers are taken off of their medication just at a time when they are naturally more defiant. I have seen many teens experience serious school and social failure after the pediatrician or family doctor prematurely took them off their medication.

-- There is a high incidence of conflicts in ADD families, especially during the teenage years. These conflicts often center around failure to perform routine chores, difficulty being trusted to obey the rules, and high levels of conflicts with parents. I have seen many teenagers sent away from home (to a residential treatment setting, boarding school or relative's house) as a way for the family to survive the turmoil.

-- Approximately 30% of ADD teens fail to finish high school. Many very intelligent young adults fail to pursue college.

-- As adults, as many as 75% have interpersonal problems; depression and low self-esteem are commonplace.

-- Juvenile convictions and adult antisocial personality disorders may occur in 23-45%.

-- Approximately 30-40% abuse alcohol and drugs, especially amphetamines and cocaine (for self-medication)

Many critics of ADD say that it is just a fad, caused by poor teachers or inept parents and that professionals are just "drugging" kids as a way to control them. Every single year for the past 15 years, I have heard that ADD is a fad. ADD is not a fad. It is not going away. As I've shown in this chapter, *left untreated, ADD has potentially serious consequences.*

WATCH FOR THE WALL

Many bright children with ADD, especially the type without hyperactivity, are not diagnosed until later in their development (if at all). They do fine for a while and then slam into failure. The Wall! Depending on intelligence, class size and knowledge level of the parents, they may not have problems until third grade, sixth grade, ninth grade or even college. I've treated some college professors who received good grades in graduate school, but still had the majority of symptoms of the disorder. They describe, however, that it took them four or five times the amount of time and effort to do as well as their peers.

My son, whose greatest difficulties were in the ninth grade, actually got straight A's in the sixth grade. He said, "In sixth grade, I knew everything that the teacher was talking about. It was easy. In ninth grade, I did not know as much and I couldn't bring myself to focus on all the material I needed to learn."

The WALL is different for each person with ADD.

CHAPTER 9

ADD In Adults

The first article on ADD in adults was written by psychiatrist Henry Mann in 1976 while he was a professor at Yale University School of Medicine. Yet, the medical community was very slow to recognize ADD in adults. It has only been since the late 1980s that professionals began speaking about ADD beyond the adolescent years. Still, in 1995, many professionals do not understand ADD in adults and often label these people as character problems, anxious, depressed or manic-depressive.

Typical Presenting Complaints
For Adults With ADD

Adults with ADD often come to our clinic with the following concerns:

1. Concerns about a child with ADD. Most adults with ADD are only diagnosed after they bring their child in for evaluation. During a thorough history, the child psychiatrists asks about family history. That is when the light goes on for many people. Child psychiatrists are best at diagnosing this disorder, because they typically see a lot of children with ADD. It was not until two of my children were diagnosed with ADD that my wife went in for an evaluation.

2. Poor school/work performance related to:
    -- deficient sustained attention to reading, paperwork, etc.,
    -- easily bored by tedious material,
    -- poor organization and planning,
    -- procrastination until deadlines are imminent,
    -- restlessness, trouble staying in a confined space (not a phobia),
    -- impulsive decision making,
    -- cannot work well independently,
    -- doesn't listen carefully to directions,
    -- frequent impulsive job changes,
    -- poor academic grades for ability,

-- often late for work/appointments,
-- frequently misplaces things,
-- trouble thinking clearly,
-- generally poor self-discipline,

3. Moodiness

4. Chronic anxiety, restlessness

5. Substance abuse

6. Uncontrolled anger at their children

7. Marital problems

8. Sleep problems

9. Financial problems

10. Impulsiveness

General Adult ADD Symptom Checklist

In addition to the checklists above, I also use the following general adult ADD checklist to help further define ADD symptoms. No ADD adult has all of the symptoms, but if you notice a strong presence of more than 20 of these symptoms, there is a strong likelihood of ADD.

Please read this list of behaviors and rate yourself (or the person who has asked you to rate him or her) on each behavior listed. Use the following scale and place the appropriate number next to the item..

0 = never
1 = rarely
2 = occasionally
3 = frequently
4 = very frequently

Past History
_____ 1. History of ADD symptoms in childhood, such as distractibility, short attention span, impulsivity or restlessness. ADD doesn't start at age 30.
_____ 2. History of not living up to potential in school or work (report cards with comments such as "not living up to potential")
_____ 3. History of frequent behavior problems in school (mostly for males)
_____ 4. History of bedwetting past age 5
_____ 5. Family history of ADD, learning problems, mood disorders or substance abuse problems

Short Attention Span/Distractibility
_____ 6. Short attention span, unless very interested in something
_____ 7. Easily distracted, tendency to drift away (although at times can be hyperfocused)
_____ 8. Lacks attention to detail, due to distractibility
_____ 9. Trouble listening carefully to directions
_____10. Frequently misplaces things
_____11. Skips around while reading, or goes to the end first, trouble staying on track
_____12. Difficulty learning new games, because it is hard to stay on track

during directions

_____13. Easily distracted during sex, causing frequent breaks or turn-offs during lovemaking

_____14. Poor listening skills

_____15. Tendency to be easily bored (tunes out)

Restlessness

_____16. Restlessness, constant motion, legs moving, fidgetiness

_____17. Has to be moving in order to think

_____18. Trouble sitting still, such as trouble sitting in one place for too long, sitting at a desk job for long periods, sitting through a movie

_____19. An internal sense of anxiety or nervousness

Impulsivity

_____20. Impulsive, in words and/or actions (spending)

_____21. Say just what comes to mind without considering its impact (tactless)

_____22. Trouble going through established channels, trouble following proper procedure, an attitude of "read the directions when all else fails"

_____23. Impatient, low frustration tolerance

_____24. A prisoner of the moment

_____25. Frequent traffic violations

_____26. Frequent, impulsive job changes

_____27. Tendency to embarrass others

_____28. Lying or stealing on impulse

Poor Organization

_____29. Poor organization and planning, trouble maintaining an organized work/living area

_____30. Chronically late or chronically in a hurry

_____31. Often have piles of stuff

_____32. Easily overwhelmed by tasks of daily living

_____33. Poor financial management (late bills, check book a mess, spending unnecessary money on late fees)

_____34. Some adults with ADD are very successful, but often only if they are surrounded with people who organize them.

Problems Getting Started and Following Through

_____35. Chronic procrastination or trouble getting started

_____36. Starting projects but not finishing them, poor follow through

_____37. Enthusiastic beginnings but poor endings

_____38. Spends excessive time at work because of inefficiencies

_____39. Inconsistent work performance

Negative Internal Feelings

_____40. Chronic sense of underachievement, feeling you should be much further along in your life than you are

_____41. Chronic problems with self-esteem

_____42. Sense of impending doom

_____42. Mood swings

_____43. Negativity

_____44. Frequent feeling of demoralization or that things won't work out for you

Relational Difficulties

_____45. Trouble sustaining friendships or intimate relationships, promiscuity

_____46. Trouble with intimacy

_____47. Tendency to be immature

_____48. Self-centered; immature interests

_____49. Failure to see others' needs or activities as important

_____50. Lack of talking in a relationship

_____51. Verbally abusive to others

_____52. Proneness to hysterical outburst

_____53. Avoids group activities

_____54. Trouble with authority

Short Fuse

_____55. Quick responses to slights that are real or imagined

_____56. Rage outbursts, short fuse

Frequent Search For High Stimulation

_____57. Frequent search for high stimulation (bungee jumping, gambling, race track, high stress jobs, ER doctors, doing many things at once, etc.)

_____58. Tendency to seek conflict, be argumentative or to start disagreements for the fun of it

Tendency To Get Stuck (thoughts or behaviors)
____59. Tendency to worry needlessly and endlessly
____60. Tendency toward addictions (food, alcohol, drugs, work)

Switches Things Around
____61. Switches around numbers, letters or words
____62. Turn words around in conversations

Writing/Fine Motor Coordination Difficulties
____63. Poor writing skills (hard to get information from brain to pen)
____64. Poor handwriting, often prints
____65. Coordination difficulties

The Harder I Try The Worse It Gets
____66. Performance becomes worse under pressure.
____67. Test anxiety, or during tests your mind tends to go blank
____68. The harder you try, the worse it gets
____69. Work or schoolwork deteriorates under pressure
____70. Tendency to turn off or become stuck when asked questions in social situations
____71. Falls asleep or becomes tired while reading

Sleep/Wake Difficulties
____72. Difficulties falling asleep, may be due to too many thoughts at night
____73. Difficulty coming awake (may need coffee or other stimulant or activity before feeling fully awake)

Low Energy
____74. Periods of low energy, especially early in the morning and in the afternoon
____75. Frequently feeling tired

Sensitive To Noise Or Touch
____76. Startles easily
____77. Sensitive to touch, clothes, noise and light

Total Score: _____ (more than 20 with a score of three or more indicates a strong tendency toward ADD. Items 1, 6, and 7 are essential to make the diagnosis)

One of the most common ways I diagnose ADD in adults is when parents reluctantly tell me that they have tried child's medication and that they found it very helpful. They report it helped them concentrate for longer periods of time. They became more organized and were less impulsive. Trying your child's medication is not something I recommend!

Predictors of a Positive Outcome

In many research studies on ADD, the following qualities seem to be the best predictors of a positive outcome.

** intelligence

** higher socioeconomic status

** low degree of aggressiveness and oppositional behavior (best single predictor of a good outcome is low aggressiveness, one-third of aggressive children get abused)

** positive peer relationships

** emotional stability

** few parental problems, or if the parents have ADD, they in treatment

** getting appropriate treatment interventions for a long enough period of time

CHAPTER 10

What Causes ADD

There are many theories about what causes ADD. The following items seem to be the most well-established causes at this time.

** high genetic transmission: (by far the most common, especially in families with a history of ADD, learning problems, depression, alcoholism or drug abuse)

** maternal alcohol or drug use (fetal alcohol/drug syndrome includes short attention span, restlessness and impulsivity)

** birth problems (lack of oxygen at birth, jaundice, etc.)

** head trauma: sometimes even minor ones can affect learning and behavior. It is important to note that many people forget about having a head trauma. The clinician needs to ask about head trauma in several different ways. I ask my patients if they have ever fallen out of a tree, off a fence, into a shallow pool, etc. It amazes me how many people who have initially denied a head injury remember it after close questioning.

** radiation exposure (very, very rare)

** meningitis/encephalitis as a preschooler

** high fevers for more than 24 hours

The underlying mechanism of ADD probably stems from neurotransmitter dysfunction (dopamine/norepinephrine) and decreased in frontal lobe cerebral blood flow. A weak arousal system in the brain stem may also be involved (probably why stimulants are helpful). Some physicians think that for some ADD is caused by delayed maturation in frontal lobes and that is why there is a group of children with ADD who outgrow their symptoms.

DIET AND A.D.D.

Over the years there has been much written about diet and ADD. From the current research only one thing is clear -- the jury is still out. The initial enthusiasm in the 1970s of the Feingold Diet has waxed and waned through the years, and the scientific literature has articles both pro and con the use of diet in treating ADD. From my own clinical experience I have not seen diet cure ADD, but I have seen it help some of the symptoms. Some children and adults do react negatively to substances like:

refined white sugar
white wheat products
milk
certain fruits (grapes and grape products)
caffeine
chemical additives and dyes (red and yellow)

Most studies report that less than 5% of ADD children, teens and adults are affected by food allergies. It is, however, often useful to pay attention to diet. If you notice a sensitivity reaction to any of the items listed above, avoid them. It can make a difference.

CHAPTER 11

Brainwave Underactivation In ADD

Research from Joel Lubar, Ph.D. at the University of Tennessee have demonstrated that children and teenagers with ADD have different electrical or brainwave patterns than "normal" control groups. When the ADD children and teenagers try to concentrate, they get an increased amount of slow brain wave activity in their frontal lobes, instead of the usual increase in fast brain wave activity that is seen in the majority of the control group.

BASIC BRAINWAVE PATTERNS

Here are the typical brainwave patterns that psychiatrists and neurologists evaluate when looking at an EEG (electroencephalogram):

delta waves (0-3 cycles per second, very slow brain waves) associated with sleep

theta waves (4-7 cycles per second, slow brain waves) associated with daydreaming and seizure activity

alpha waves (8-12 cycles per second, moderate brain waves) associated with focused relaxation

sensorimotor rhythm (12-15 cycles per second, moderate to fast brain waves) noted by some to be a protective brain rhythm against seizure activity

beta waves (16-20 cycles per second, fast brain waves) associated with concentration

For ADD, during concentration there is:

too much

theta wave activity or daydreaming brainwaves

not enough

beta wave activity or concentration brainwaves

In studying hundreds of children, teens and adults with computerized EEGs, I have seen the pattern reported by Dr. Lubar. In my experience with these patients, we study them in a resting state, as well as when they are reading, drawing, listening, performing math tasks, and playing video games. They are then given Ritalin or Dexedrine and the EEG is repeated using the same tasks. When the medications work, there is a normalization of the brainwave pattern.

CHAPTER 12

How Can I Tell If I Have ADD?

There is no single, definitive test to diagnose ADD. As we'll see, psychological tests, continuous performance tests and brain imaging studies such as SPECT and computerized EEG can be very helpful in the diagnosis, but the diagnosis for the clinical syndrome of ADD is made primarily through the history. In order for ADD to be present, the symptoms need to be present for the bulk of a person's life.

Assessment Tools

-- The history (interviews with children, parents, teachers and caregivers; for adults it may be important to talk with parents, spouses, lovers and business partners).

-- Behavior rating scales (such as the Conners Parent-Teacher Rating Scale for children and the Wender Scale for Adults) are often useful. The Conners Parent-Teacher Rating Scale is helpful in helping follow the response to treatment.

-- Psychological tests, such as the WISC-R, Matching Familiar Figures Test, Trail Making Test, etc., can be helpful. There is however, no one psychological test that is specific for ADD.

-- Often, it is best for the psychologist to watch the patient's approach to the test, looking for clues such as impulsivity in responding, distractibility and a short attention span.

-- Psychological and educational testing are often important to establish the presence or absence of concurrent learning disabilities.

-- Continuous performance tasks, such as the T.O.V.A developed by Lawrence Greenhill or the C.P.T. developed by Keith Conners, Ph.D., are another way to measure attention span and impulsivity. In these tests, you watch a computer screen and respond to appropriate signals. Prolonged response time, missed responses or incorrect responses often correlate with ADD.

-- Brain imaging studies have increased in use over the past several years, especially because the advancement in computer technology has allowed the price of the equipment to become much more affordable to local physicians and hospitals. Computerized EEG studies have been used by Joel Lubar, Ph.D. at the University of Tennessee and I have participated in the development of brain SPECT imaging in ADD in Fairfield, California.

Again, the final diagnosis of this disorder is made through the patient's clinical history.

Notes:

Part III

Windows Into The ADD Mind:

The Use of Brain SPECT IMAGING In ADD

CHAPTER 13

The Use of Brain SPECT Imaging In Evaluating And Treating ADD

Beginning in February 1991, my colleagues and I began doing brain SPECT imaging studies on patients who met the DSM-IIIR criteria for attention deficit hyperactivity disorder and attention deficit disorder without hyperactivity. Brain SPECT is a nuclear medicine study, where the person is injected with a very small amount of a radioactive compound (the level of radiation from the study is very, very small). The compound is taken up by receptor sites in the brain and provides an intricate picture of brain blood flow, which is an indirect measurement of brain metabolism.

In 1990, Alan Zametkin, M.D. from the National Institutes of Mental Health published an article in the New England Journal of Medicine on the use of PET (positron emission tomography) studies, also a nuclear imaging study, in ADD. He demonstrated that adults with ADD had decreased brain activity in their frontal lobes in response to an intellectual challenge, rather than the expected increase in activity that was seen in normal "control" adults.

This information was consistent with Dr. Lubar's work with computerized EEG brain wave studies on children and adolescent patients with attention deficit hyperactivity disorder. His studies found that when these patients performed a concentration task, such as reading or copying figures, there was an increase in frontal lobe theta activity (slow brain wave activity) rather than the expected decrease in frontal lobe slow wave activity that is found in normal controls.

Both of these findings are consistent with frontal lobe deactivation in response to an intellectual stress in children, adolescents and adults with Attention Deficit Disorders. The more these people try to concentrate, it appears, the worse thinking and concentrating becomes for them. This is a particularly interesting finding in light of the clinical fact that ADD children are often very "stimulation seeking." It is not unusual at all in the history gathered from the parents to find that these children are continually getting other people angry or upset with them. Could this be an attempt for them to try to stimulate their own brains? For the person to treat himself to feel more normal?

In my opinion, brain SPECT imaging has the potential to be clinically more useful than both PET studies and computerized EEG. Opposed to computerized EEG, SPECT gives a three-dimensional picture of the cortex of the brain as well as the deeper structures of the brain, whereas computerized EEG depends solely on scalp readings.

PET, which is a direct measure of metabolic activity, would seem the most sensitive study of all of cerebral metabolism. However, with the expense being approximately twice that of a SPECT study, the limited availability of PET equipment (SPECT equipment is found in most community hospitals), and the requirement for an intra-arterial line for the procedure (as opposed to an intravenous line for SPECT), I feel research with SPECT has the greatest potential for everyday clinical utility. With advances in technology, SPECT resolution is becoming comparable to that of PET studies.

In studying psychiatric patients with brain SPECT imaging, researchers have found brain blood flow patterns for different psychiatric conditions. Some clinicians have reservations about the use of SPECT in children, feeling it may be unsafe. The radiation exposure from SPECT is equivalent to a pelvic x-ray. Nuclear medicine, as a specialty, has been doing studies on children for over thirty years without untoward effects. Having an unresponsive or poorly responsive psychiatric condition has many more risks than the risk of low dose radiation exposure engendered by a SPECT scan.

In 1993, I presented our findings at the annual meeting of the American Psychiatric Association and the annual meeting of the Society for Biological Psychiatry. Our work was also reported in Clinical Psychiatry News (a newspaper that goes to every psychiatrist in the country) and on the Discovery Channel on a program called Next Steps.

In performing SPECT studies on hundreds of children, teenagers and adults with ADD, I have seen the same frontal lobe "turn off" that has been reported by Drs. Zametkin and Lubar. When people with ADD try to concentrate, the frontal lobes of their brain (which control attention span, judgment, impulse control and motivation) decrease in activity. When normal control groups do concentration tasks, there is increased activity in this part of the brain. So, the harder these people try, the worse it gets for them.

When I explain this phenomena to children, I use the following illustration:

"When you have ADD, it is like putting your foot on the gas pedal in a car; you expect the car to go faster but it doesn't. It actually goes slower! This is a very important point to remember." ADD is a physical, neurobiological disorder.

It must be emphasized that brain SPECT imaging in most clinical settings is still considered a research tool. In order to utilize the technology effectively, it is important to have a sophisticated camera (we used a triple-headed camera; most SPECT cameras are still single headed and provide less resolution), a nuclear medicine physician skilled in reading brain studies for psychiatric or functional reasons, and a psychiatrist who understands how to properly utilize the technology. It is not common to find all of these ingredients in the same clinical setting. I present my work here for the purpose of demonstrating several things. First, I want to clearly demonstrate that ADD is a neurobiological disorder. Second, the use of SPECT has helped to shed light on the various subtypes of ADD. Third, SPECT has been helpful in very difficult cases, often showing me that there were 2 or 3 different problems occurring at once. Lastly, family SPECT studies provide another piece of evidence that ADD has genetic underpinnings.

From the research with brain SPECT studies, my colleagues and I have seen five different brain patterns associated with ADD. You'll note that I report the results of two studies on each person: a resting study (done while the person was in a resting state) and an intellectual stress study (done while the person was doing a series of concentration tasks, such as random math problems). In evaluating ADD, it is essential to look at a working brain.

I. Attention Deficit Disorder with <u>Frontal Lobe "TURN OFF"</u>, without other findings (Classic ADD which often responds to stimulant medications alone)

History:

Joe was a 7-year-old male with history of increased activity level, short attention span, impulsiveness, failure to finish work, intrusiveness with other children and oppositional behavior. The parents had Joe evaluated by a developmental pediatrician who thought Joe had mild ADD. Parents then brought him to me for a second opinion. I concurred with ADD diagnosis, but parents refused to use medication.

The parents attended a parenting group that I taught, which helped Joe's behavior at home. At school the next year, however, the teacher reported his behavior was difficult and disruptive. Joe didn't finish assignments and bothered other children. The parents and teacher had a poor relationship. The parents were upset the teacher couldn't keep Joe under better "control." At that point a brain SPECT was ordered to document if there was an underlying biological problem which would further encourage the use of appropriate medication.

Joe's SPECT Scan
(horizontal view)

FRONT OF THE BRAIN

LEFT 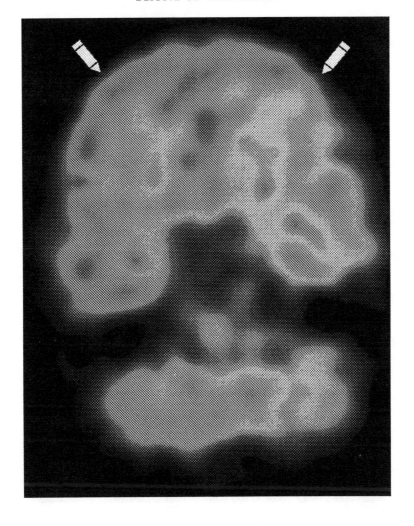 RIGHT

BACK OF THE BRAIN

Baseline study -- normal
(notice full activity in frontal lobes at the top of the scan)

75

Joe's SPECT Scan
(horizontal view)

FRONT OF THE BRAIN

LEFT 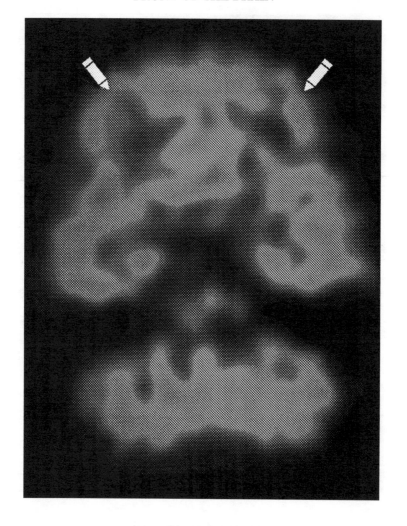 RIGHT

BACK OF THE BRAIN

Intellectual stress study:
marked decreased in frontal lobe
activity compared to baseline

Joe's SPECT Scan
(side view)

TOP OF THE BRAIN

FRONT 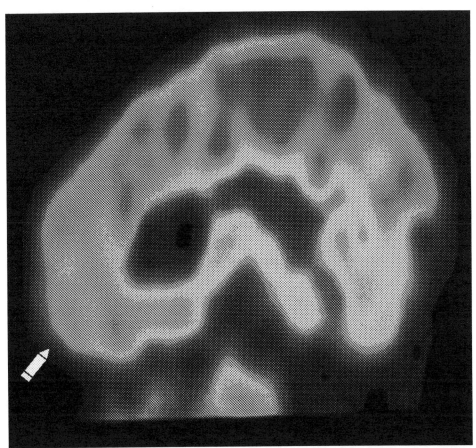 BACK

BOTTOM OF THE BRAIN

Baseline study -- normal
(notice full activity in frontal lobes at the left of the scan)

Joe's SPECT Scan
(side view)

TOP OF THE BRAIN

FRONT 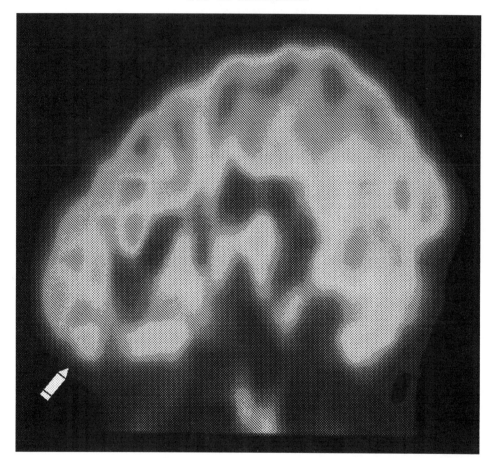 BACK

BOTTOM OF THE BRAIN

Intellectual stress study
marked decreased in frontal lobe activity
compared to baseline

78

Follow Up:

The brain SPECT Scan result convinced the parents of the biological basis of Joe's problems and they agreed to a trial of methylphenidate (Ritalin). The child had a markedly positive response. He was more on task at school, finished more of his work and got along much better with other children. The parents and teacher had an improved relationship which sustained through 24 months.

II. Attention Deficit Disorder with <u>Temporal Lobe Dysfunction</u> (often responds best to anticonvulsant medication)

History:

Kris was a 12 year old male with a history of oppositional behavior, emotional outbursts, increased activity level, short attention span, impulsiveness, school problems, frequent lying and aggressive behavior.

At age 6 Kris was placed on methylphenidate (Ritalin) but he became more aggressive and it was stopped. He was admitted to a psychiatric hospital in Alaska at age 8 and given the diagnosis of depression and started on desipramine (Norpramin). At age 12, he had been seen for several years of psychotherapy by a psychoanalysis in the Napa Valley, and his parents were seen in collateral sessions as well.

The psychiatrist frequently blamed the mother as the "biggest part of Kris' problem." He told her that if only she would get into psychotherapy and deal with her childhood issues then Kris' problems would go away. Kris' behavior escalated to the point where he was aggressive and uncontrollable at home. He was rehospitalized.

I was on call the weekend Kris was hospitalized. To bond with the kids, sometimes I play football with them. Kris was on my team. Every single play he tried to cheat. When we were on defense, he would move the ball back several feet and then turn around to look at me, as if he were trying to get me angry. I refused to play his ADD game of "get the adult angry".

Kris' SPECT Scan
(front on view)

TOP OF THE BRAIN

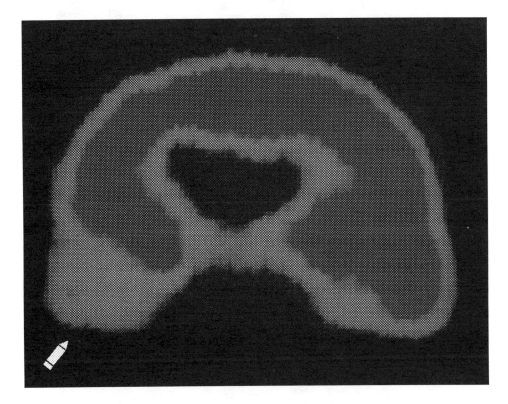

LEFT

RIGHT

BOTTOM OF THE BRAIN

Baseline study
defect in the left temporal lobe
(light area indicates decreased activity)

Kris' SPECT Scan
(horizontal view)

FRONT OF THE BRAIN

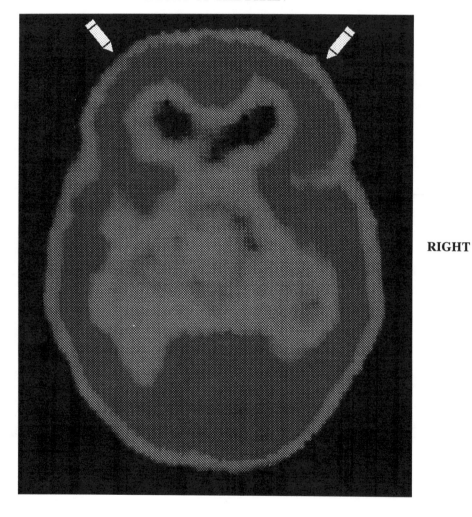

LEFT

RIGHT

BACK OF THE BRAIN

Baseline study
(cannot see temporal lobe defect from this view, but
notice full activity in frontal lobes at the top of the scan)

Kris' SPECT Scan
(horizontal view)

FRONT OF THE BRAIN

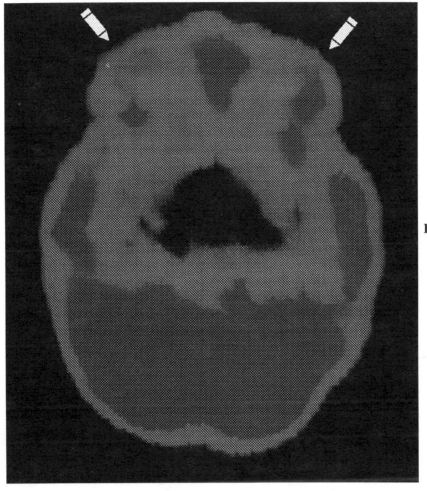

LEFT   **RIGHT**

BACK OF THE BRAIN

Intellectual stress study:
notice marked decreased activity in
frontal lobes compared to baseline

Follow Up:

Kris was placed on carbamazepine (Tegretol) at a therapeutic level. Within a month he was a dramatically different child. He was more compliant, his school work improved and he is doing better with other children. His mother no longer looks like "the problem." The positive response has held for 28 months.

Note: In my experience, temporal lobe problems coincide with spaciness, periods of confusion, panic or fear for no reason, visual illusions, violence and suicidal behavior (especially with left-sided temporal lobe problems)

III. Attention Deficit Disorder with <u>decreased activity across the whole brain surface, often accompanied by increased activity in the limbic system</u> (typically responds best to antidepressants)

History:

William was a 12-year-old male with a history of oppositional behavior, emotional outbursts, fire setting, erratic school behavior, short attention span, impulsiveness, and irritability.

William had been seen in psychotherapy for a year by a child psychiatrist. He was tried on methylphenidate (Ritalin) and magnesium pemoline (Cylert) with little response. After a fire-setting episode he was hospitalized.

William's SPECT Scan
(horizontal view)

FRONT OF THE BRAIN

LEFT 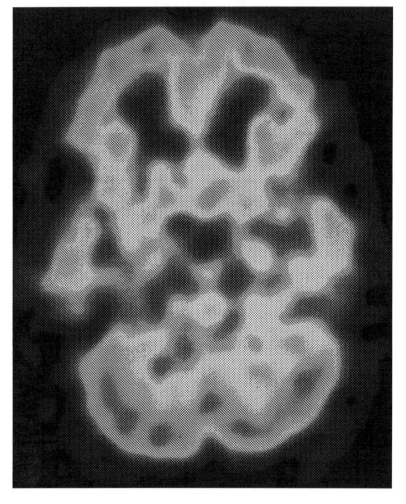 RIGHT

BACK OF THE BRAIN

Baseline study
marked decreased activity across
the whole brain surface

William's SPECT Scan
(horizontal view)

FRONT OF THE BRAIN

LEFT 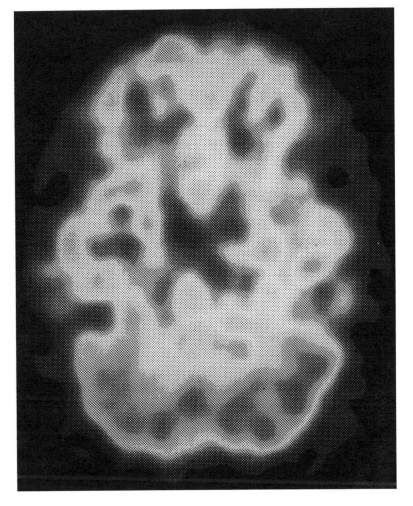 RIGHT

BACK OF THE BRAIN

Intellectual stress study
further decreased activity across the whole brain,
especially in the prefrontal cortices

Follow Up:

William was placed on desipramine (an antidepressant). Thirteen months later he remains markedly improved. There have been no fire- setting incidents. He was much more compliant and less emotional. His school performance was better than ever before.

IV. Attention Deficit Disorder with increased activity in the <u>top, middle aspects of the frontal lobes</u> (this pattern is reported in the scientific literature in patients who have obsessive-compulsive disorders)

History:

17-year-old Bob was admitted to a psychiatric hospital after he became withdrawn and depressed. Bob had a long history of emotional outbursts, erratic school performance, periods of social withdrawal and getting thoughts "stuck" in his brain. His parents reported that once Bob got a thought in his head he was unable to let it go. In fact, his mother said that he would follow her around the house for hours asking her the same question. Additionally, he was restless, had a short attention span, was impulsive and very distractible. His mother was also hospitalized for depression with obsessive features.

Bob's SPECT Scan
(front on)

TOP OF THE BRAIN

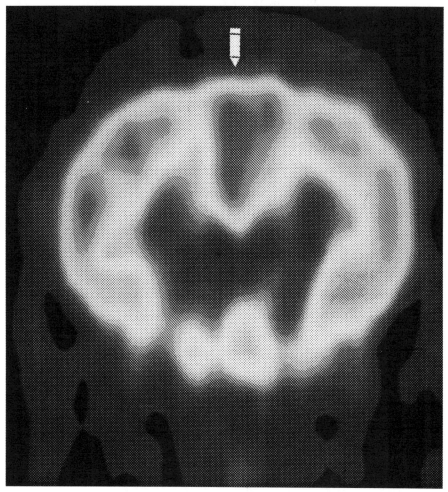

LEFT

RIGHT

BOTTOM OF THE BRAIN

Baseline study
increased activity in the top, middle portion
of his frontal lobes

90

Bob's SPECT Scan
(side view)

TOP OF THE BRAIN

FRONT   BACK

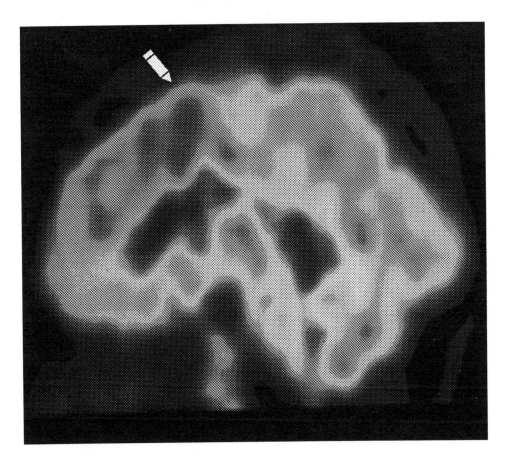

BOTTOM OF THE BRAIN

Baseline study
increased activity in the top,
middle portion of his frontal lobes

91

Bob's intellectual stress study showed intensification of the increased activity in the top, middle portion of his frontal lobes, along with marked decreased in frontal lobe activity compared to baseline.

Follow Up:

The SPECT Scan result and clinical history directed us to place Bob on the anti-obsessive medication clomipramine (Anafranil).

Seven months later, Bob was happier, more social and doing better in school than he had in several years. He reports actually being able to sit down and do his homework in "half the time it used to take."

V. Attention Deficit Disorder with <u>decreased frontal lobe activity at rest</u> (even though these children and adults activate their frontal lobes with intellectual stress, at rest they have decreased activity in their frontal lobes relative to the rest of their brain.)

History:

Eight-year-old Philip had problems with hyperactivity, distractibility, impulsivity and restlessness since before starting school. He frequently was engaged in battles with his parents over his refusal to do what was asked of him. His mother said that because of Philip's continually irritating and defiant behavior, she frequently yelled at him, even though she promised herself that she wouldn't. Philip and his family spent two years in psychotherapy without benefit.

Phillip's SPECT Scan
(side view)

TOP OF THE BRAIN

FRONT 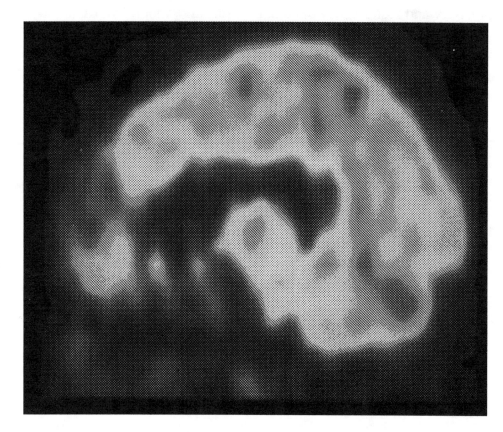 BACK

BOTTOM OF THE BRAIN

Baseline study
marked decreased activity in the frontal lobes.

Phillip's intellectual stress study showed a mild increase in activity in the frontal lobe compared to baseline.

Follow Up:

Philip was placed on low dose methylphenidate (Ritalin) and had a markedly positive response, doing better at home and at school over the next sixteen months.

SPECT FAMILY STUDY:

**Depression, ADD and
Obsessive-Compulsive Disorder**

History:

Before she came to see me, Celina, 36, had been depressed for ten years, following the birth of her first child. Her symptoms included significant irritability, crying spells, sleeplessness and weight loss. She also had problems concentrating and she was unable to manage her two children. Her condition was brought to a crisis when she attempted suicide after separating from her husband. She was initially seen by a psychiatrist who started her on medication for depression, but this had little effect on her. She then came to see me. I treated her with psychotherapy and a different antidepressant. The treatment helped her feel more positive and less irritable. Several months later, she decided that she "should be stronger than the depression" and took herself off the medication. Within several days her depression worsened, but she was resistant to restarting her medication. She told me, "I don't want to have to rely on medication to feel well."

In an effort to demonstrate to Celina that her depression was, at least in part, biological and that her medication was an important part of treatment, I ordered a brain SPECT study. Celina's SPECT study revealed marked decreased frontal lobe activity and increased activity in her limbic system, which fit with her underlying depression. In addition, it showed striking overactivity in the top, middle portion of her frontal lobes. This finding is often seen in people with obsessive compulsive disorder.

With this information I asked her more directly about obsessive thoughts and compulsive symptoms. In fact, Celina was perfectionistic at home, she had obsessive negative thoughts and she tearfully remarked, "You mean my husband was right when he said it was strange that I had to have all the shirts buttoned a certain way and put just so in the drawer."

She then told me about her eight-year-old daughter, Laura, who had rituals. Before Laura would enter a new room she would run a finger under her nose and lick her lips. She also became obsessed with locking doors and would frequently lock her brother and sister out of the house.

Another psychiatrist had been seeing Celina's ten-year-old son, Samuel, for a school and behavior problems. He had been diagnosed with Attention Deficit Disorder and was taking a stimulant medication, but it had little effect for him. One of Celina's concerns about Samuel was that once he got a thought in his mind he would be unable to let it go. He would follow her around the house for two and a half hours asking her the same questions she had already answered.

A brain SPECT study was then done on both children. Interestingly, they showed the same overactivity in the top, middle portion of their frontal lobes, suggesting an obsessive-compulsive component to their problems.

Celina's SPECT Study
(front on view)

TOP OF THE BRAIN

LEFT

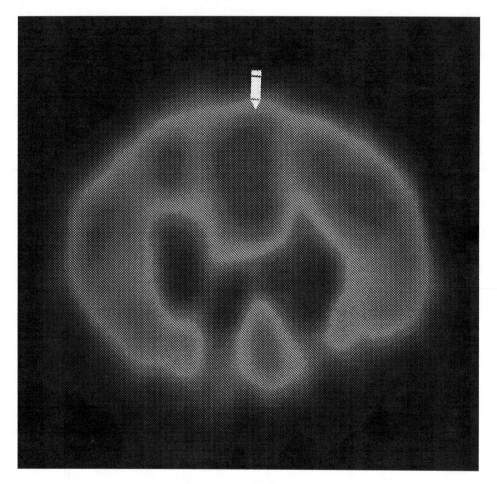

RIGHT

BOTTOM OF THE BRAIN

Celina's baseline study
increased activity in the top, middle
portion of her frontal lobes

Laura's SPECT Study
(front on view)

TOP OF THE BRAIN

LEFT 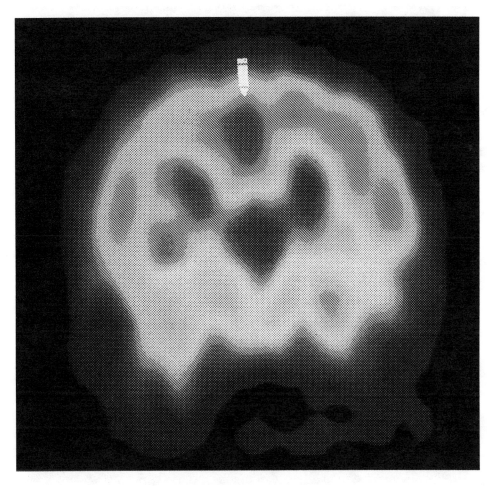 RIGHT

BOTTOM OF THE BRAIN

Laura's baseline study
increased activity in the top, middle
portion of her frontal lobes

99

Samuel's SPECT Study
(front on view)

TOP OF THE BRAIN

LEFT 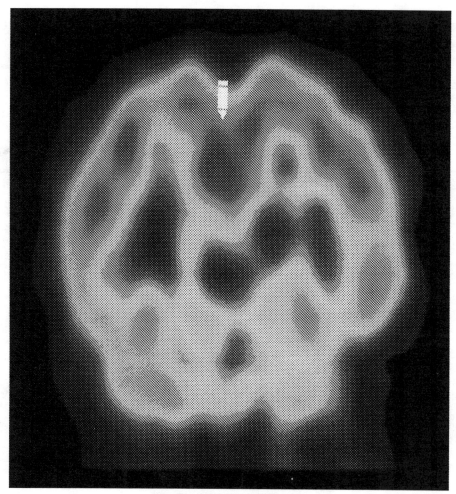 RIGHT

BOTTOM OF THE BRAIN

Samuel's baseline study
increased activity in the top, middle
portion of his frontal lobes

Of note, Celina deactivated her frontal lobes when she tried to concentrate, as did Samuel. Celina was labeled as an underachiever in school and also had difficulty completing projects. Laura, on the other hand, activated her frontal lobes and was not noted to have any school or concentration problems.

Follow up:

Based on this information, the mother, Celina, was placed on the antidepressant Prozac (fluoxetine) to decrease her depression and help lessen her obsessive thinking and compulsive behaviors. Prozac is a very effective treatment for obsessive-compulsive disorder. She had a dramatically positive response and reported that she was not bothered when things weren't "just so." She also said that it was the first time in ten years that she felt "herself." The SPECT study also convinced her that her condition was at least, in part, biological and not her fault or the result of a weak will, which allowed her to take her medication for a longer period of time.

With this information, Samuel's psychiatrist stopped the stimulant medication and started him on Prozac as well. Within several weeks, his behavior normalized and he had a remarkable improvement in school, making the honor roll for the first time in his life. Several months later, Laura was also placed on Prozac and her ritualistic behavior markedly diminished.

Certainly, the family dynamics in this family operated on many levels. The mother's depression contributed to the anxiety and behavior problems in her children and the abnormal brain metabolism in the children probably added to their difficult behavior which further stressed the mother. The family dynamics improved significantly after the mother and the children were treated with the appropriate medication and psychotherapy.

Increased activity in the top, middle part of the frontal lobes is the consistent SPECT finding in obsessive compulsive disorder. Of interest, it is reported in the psychosurgery literature that surgically interrupting the nerve fibers in this area, a procedure known as a cingulotomy, can often alleviate the symptoms of obsessive compulsive disorder.

The SPECT studies we've done have confirmed the work of others suggesting that ADD is a problem where the brain is underactivated, rather than overstimulated as many have thought. This makes sense, as we know that stimulant medications help these children and adults.

PART IV

THE DAY-TO-DAY IMPACT OF ADD

CHAPTER 14

ADD And Ringing Pavlov's Bell

Having decreased activity in the front part of the brain is likely a very uncomfortable state of mind. Because of this, I postulate that many ADD children, teens and adults "unconsciously" seek stimulation. Hyperactivity, restlessness and humming are common ways these people may try to stimulate themselves. Another way I have seen these people "try to turn on their brains" is by causing turmoil. If they can get their parents or their spouses to yell at them that might increase activity in their frontal lobes and help them to feel more tuned in. Again, this is not a conscious phenomenon. These people do not know that they are doing this to get turned on. But, it seems many ADD people become addicted to the turmoil. They repeatedly get others upset with them even though there is no conscious benefit to their behavior. This is "Pavlovian," or conditioned behavior.

I once treated a man who would quietly stand behind a corner in his house and jump out and scare his wife when she walked by. He liked the charge he got out of her screams. I have also treated many ADD adults and children who seemed driven to get their animals upset by rough play or teasing them.

The parents of ADD children commonly report that the kids are experts at getting them upset. One mother told me that when she wakes up in the morning, she promises herself that she won't yell or get upset with her 8-year-old son. Yet, invariably, by the time he is off for school, there have been at least three fights and both of them feel terrible. When I explained the child's unconscious need for stimulation to the mother, she stopped yelling at him. When parents stop providing the negative stimulation (yelling, spanking, lecturing, etc.) these children decrease the behaviors. Whenever you feel like screaming at one of these kids, talk as softly as you can. At least in that way you're breaking their addiction to turmoil and lowering your own blood pressure.

CHAPTER 15

The Impact Of ADD On Relationships

As a child, teen or adult, ADD often has a negative impact on a person's ability to interact with others. Here are some of the reasons:

Social isolation:

Many people with ADD have failed in relationships so much in the past that they don't want to experience the pain anymore. Their outrageous behavior often ostracizes them from their peer group.

Teasing:

The person with ADD often appears different and is teased by others. Additionally, their impulsivity causes them to tease others, sometimes to the point where the other person becomes very upset.

Fighting:

Fighting is typical for many people with ADD. It may be related to impulsivity (saying things without thinking), stimulation-seeking behavior, misperceptions, rage outbursts and chronically low self-esteem.

Misperceptions:

Misperceptions often causes serious problems in the relationships. Often the parent or spouse of an ADD person has to spend an inordinate amount of time correcting misperceptions that lead to disagreements. Once, on the night before I was leaving on a business trip, I told my wife that I was going to miss her. She heard my words as "I'm not going to miss you" and she was angry at me for the rest of the night.

Distractibility:

Due to distractibility, conversations are often cut short or left uncompleted, leaving the other person feeling unimportant.

Problems Taking Turns:

The ADD person's need to have what they want right away often causes problems in situations where they need to take turns, such as in conversations or games.

Speaking Without Thinking:

This is perhaps the most damaging problem with ADD in relationships. Just because a person has a thought doesn't mean that it is accurate or that or that they necessarily believe it. Many people with ADD just say what comes to mind. They then get stuck in defending these statements, which causes further problems.

Problems Completing Chores:

This leads to many resentments, arguments and frustrations.

Difficulty Playing or Being Quiet:

Often the level of activity or noise created by the ADD person causes frustration and irritability in others.

Sensitivity to Noise:

When the ADD person is sensitive to noise, they often need to escape from others to feel calm or peaceful inside.

Sensitivity to Touch:

When the person is sensitive to touch, they often shy away from affection. This can harm a relationship, especially if the person's partner wants or needs affection.

Excessive Talking:

Sometimes people with ADD talk, just to talk, and end up not saying much. This irritates others, because if they don't listen, then the ADD person becomes upset.

Lack of Talking:

The partners of some ADD people complain that there is little talking in the relationship. "He seems turned off when he comes home" is a common complaint. Often parents will ask these children about their day and the only response they'll get is "fine" or "OK."

Disorganization:

This causes problems in a relationship because the ADD person often doesn't live up to their part of the chores or agreements.

Takes High Risks/Thrill Seeking:

This type of behavior worries the parents, partners or friends of the ADD person. Friends often feel pressured to go along with dangerous behavior, causing a rift in the relationship.

Easily Frustrated/Emotional/Moody

Many family members of ADD children, teens and adults have told me that they never know what to expect from the ADD person. "One minute she's happy, the next minute she's screaming," is a common complaint. Small amounts of stress may trigger off huge explosions.

Tantrums/Rage Outbursts

Some studies have reported that up to 85% of people with ADD have rage outbursts, often with little provocation. After this occurs several times in a relationship, the parent, partner or friend becomes "gun shy" and starts to withdraw from the person. Untreated ADD is often involved in abusive relationships.

Low Self-Esteem

When people do not feel good about themselves, it impairs their ability to relate to others. They have difficulty taking compliments or getting outside of themselves to truly understand the other person. The brain filters information coming in from the environment. When the brain's filter (self-esteem) is negative, people tend to only see the negative and ignore any positive. Many partners of ADD people complain that when they give their partner a compliment, they find a way to make it look like they have just been criticized.

Looking for Turmoil:

This is a common complaint of people living with someone who has ADD. They say that the person looks for trouble. Rather than ignoring a minor incident, he or she focuses on it and has difficulty letting it go. Things in an ADD house do not remain peaceful for long periods of time.

Chronic Anxiety or Restlessness:

As mentioned above, ADD people often feel restless or anxious. This often causes them to search for ways to relax. They may use excessive sex, food or alcohol to try to calm themselves. I treated one man who had had sex with his girlfriend over 500 times in the last year of their relationship. She left him, because she felt that their relationship was only based upon sex.

Failure to See Others' Needs:

Many people with ADD have trouble getting outside of themselves to see the emotional needs of others. They are often labeled as spoiled, immature or self-centered.

Lack of Learning from the Past:

Often people with ADD engage in repetitive, negative arguments with others. They seem not to learn from the interpersonal mistakes from their past and repeat them again and again.

Chronic Procrastination

The ADD person often waits until the very last minute to get things done (bills, buying birthday, anniversary or Christmas gifts, etc.). This irritates those around them.

CHAPTER 16

The Impact Of ADD On Families

ADD often causes serious problems in families. I have seen "caring" families fall apart because of the turmoil caused by having an ADD child. I have also seen many divorces between people who "truly loved each other" because of the stress of one or both partners having ADD. Many of the issues listed in the "Impact of ADD on Relationships" section apply here. Here are several other important issues to consider.

Drive Toward Turmoil:

ADD children and teenagers are often experts at getting their parents to yell at them. As I mentioned above, the ADD person often has decreased activity in their frontal lobes and they "unconsciously" seek stimulation to feel more awake or alert. In a family, this takes on many forms, such as temper tantrums, noise and high activity.

Parental Splitting:

ADD kids may also be skilled at getting their parents to fight with each other. Splitting parental authority gives children and teenagers too much power and increases the turmoil. Often the scenario is that the mother will blame the father for being "too absent" or "too harsh," and the father will blame the mother for being "too inconsistent" and "too soft." Of course, this goes both ways. I have seen many couples separate, in part, to stop the turmoil they lived in at home.

Negative Expectations:

In families with an ADD child, teen or adult there is often the expectation that there will be problems, so people begin to avoid each other or predict their will be problems. For example, a mother recently told me she expected that her ADD husband wouldn't finish the dinner dishes as he promised. Before he even had a chance to do them, she "resentfully" cleaned them. She was angry at him for the rest of the night, even though she didn't give him a chance to be helpful.

Feelings of Parents

Denial -- "There's nothing wrong with the child! He only needs more time, more attention, more discipline, more love, a better teacher, a better school, a firmer mother, a father who is more available." These are common excuses parents make to deny that any problem exists. Admitting that there is a problem is often so painful that many parents go years and years without seeking help. Denial can seriously harm a child or teen's chances for success!

Grief -- There is often a grieving process that occurs in a family with an untreated ADD person. The parents or spouse often feel the loss of having a "normal" child, teen or spouse and end up feeling very sad that the situation is not as they expected it would be.

On Guard -- For many parents, living with an ADD child is like being in a war zone. They have to be constantly on guard that the child won't run out into the street, won't break something at the store or won't run off at a park. This chronic watchfulness causes much internal tension for parents.

Guilt -- Guilt is a significant issue for many parents of ADD children. The turmoil that an ADD child, teen or adult causes often brings on bad feelings. Parents or spouses are not "supposed" to have bad feelings toward people they love and so end up burdened by feelings of guilt. In the treatment section, I'll discuss how to break the cycle of guilt.

Anger -- Anger at the teachers, doctors, day care workers and the other parent is common in parents with an ADD child. The levels of frustration are so high in these families that people look for someone on whom to blow off steam.

Envy -- "Why can't we have normal kids? We didn't do anything to deserve the turmoil. It's not fair."

Blame -- "You spoil him. How's he ever going to learn if you do everything for him? You're too soft on her. You never say a kind word to him. If only you would be home more than we wouldn't have these problems with her." Blame is very destructive and rarely if ever helpful. Yet, it is all too common in ADD families.

Isolation -- "Everyone thinks I'm a bad parent. No one else has these problems. I can't go anywhere with him, I'm stuck at home." Feelings of isolation are very common. Many parents of ADD children feel that they are the only ones in the world who have these problems. Joining a support group can be very helpful for these people.

Bargaining -- "Maybe she'll be OK if we put her in a new school. Maybe if we put him in outside activities his attitude will improve. Maybe if I leave his father, we'll all feel better." Many parents of ADD children attribute their problems to outside forces and feel that making radical life style changes will help. Without the right treatment, however, these changes are rarely helpful.

Depression -- "I'm a failure as a parent. I've failed my child. I have no business raising children. I should go to work and leave him with a sitter. I'm so tired that I can't do this anymore." The physical and emotional drain of having an ADD child can often trigger off a significant depression. Watch your moods.

Sibling Issues:

Children with ADD often irritate their siblings to the point of causing tears, anger or fighting. Siblings develop negative feelings toward the ADD child because they are often embarrassed by their outrageous behavior at school or with friends.

Since ADD, for the most part, is a genetic disorder, it is more likely that siblings may also have features of ADD. Having two or more members of a family with untreated ADD can completely disorganize the family.

Often times in families with an ADD child, there is an identified "good" child and a "bad" (ADD) child. Because the parents' self-esteem is so damaged by having an unrecognized ADD child they will often avoid the ADD child and focus a lot of positive energy on the other child and think that they are more "perfect" than they really are. This causes resentment in the ADD child. It also causes the "perfect" child to subvert and progress that the ADD child might make. Corey and Sarah were an example of this "sibling subversion." Here's an example:

Corey, 9, had a severe case of ADD. He would throw three-hour temper tantrums, had problems nearly every day in school, and was chronically non-compliant with his mother. Six-year-old Sarah, with long, curly, red hair, was her mother's angel. She could do no wrong. With treatment, Corey began to significantly improve. But, in therapy, Corey told me that his little sister was "flipping him off" with her middle finger. When he told his mother, she did not believe him. "Sarah wouldn't do that, she's too sweet." I told the mother to secretly watch them when they were playing together. Sure enough, Sarah was using her middle finger to drive Corey crazy. She was having difficulty losing her place in the family as the "perfect" child and she had a stake in Corey remaining a problem.

Feelings of Brothers and Sisters:

Embarrassment -- just as parents are blamed by neighbors for unacceptable behavior of their child, so brothers and sisters are often held responsible or ridiculed by their peers for the actions of their ADD sibling

Anger -- an ADD child can evoke intense emotions in his brother or sister.

Resentment -- a sibling may feel very resentful at being labeled "weirdo sister" or having a child come up and say, "Hey, do you know what your brother did?"

Put-Upon -- they feel urged to include the ADD child in their play and free time activities. He or she often has few friends of their own and it's natural for parents to seek relief.

Guilt -- like parents, siblings often feel guilty for emotions they harbor. They care deeply in spite of the behavior they live with.

Out of Control -- brothers and sisters find it difficult to engage the ADD child in play without constant struggles over rules and issues of control. They may strike out at the ADD child as a result of being constantly frustrated.

Jealousy -- siblings often question the double standards that exist in the rules that they are governed by. The ADD child is often rewarded when the behavior does not warrant it as a way of pacifying him or her at the time.

CHAPTER 17

The Impact Of ADD On School

Whether for children, teenagers or adults, ADD has a powerful negative impact on a person's ability to do well in school. Except for classes that are small or highly interesting, many people with ADD have significant problems. Here is a list of common school problems.

Restlessness:

The hyperactivity that often accompanies ADD in childhood causes obvious problems: the child is restless, out of his or her seat, irritating other kids (not to mention the teacher) and causing turmoil and disruption in his or her path. In teens and adults, the restlessness of ADD often distracts others in class who notice the constant movement (i.e., legs shaking, shifting body posture in seats).

Short Attention Span and Distractibility:

Having a short attention span and being easily distracted affects nearly every aspect of school. This will affect a student's ability to follow teachers in lectures, participate in small groups and perform consistently on tests. The short attention span often causes the ADD student's attention to wander while reading or performing class assignments, causing them to take an inordinate amount of time to finish tasks. Distractibility also may get ADD students in trouble, as they tend to be in everyone else's business.

Impulsiveness:

Impulsiveness causes serious school problems. Blurting out answers in class, responding impulsively on quizzes or tests and saying things without thinking are typical. I've treated many people with ADD who were "tactless" in how they responded to their teachers or professors. One teenager said to her teacher, "You're a lousy teacher! I don't know why you explain things like that, but the other teachers know how to explain things a lot better than you do." All of us have had that thought about certain teachers at one time or another. Most people, however, would never blurt out a statement like that because it would hurt the teacher's feelings and harm their relationship. But with ADD, you engage your mouth before you engage your brain.

Procrastination:

Many people with ADD wait until the last minute to complete their tasks for school. If it isn't the night before, they cannot get their brain upset enough to get their work done. Many parents have told me about the constant fights they have with their children or teens about starting projects early and working on them overtime, rather than the night before. Many adults have told me that they never did term papers in school or they used amphetamines the night before the work was due to get it done. Procrastination in school caused the work to be done poorly or for it be left undone or incomplete.

Trouble Shifting Attention:

As I mentioned above, there is a group of people with ADD who have trouble shifting their attention from thing to thing. They have a tendency to get "stuck" or overfocus. This characteristic can be particularly troublesome in school. Getting stuck on an idea early in a lecture may cause the student to miss the information for much of the lecture. Taking notes for these students is often a disaster. Note taking requires a constant shifts in attention: from paying attention to the lecture, to the paper, from the lecture to the paper, from the lecture to the paper, etc.

Forgetfulness:

This symptom often upsets the parents and teachers of ADD students. Forgetting to bring home books, leaving clothes at school, and not turning in homework assignments that were completed are common complaints.

Learning Disabilities:

Learning difficulties and disabilities are very common in people with ADD. It is essential to recognize and treat these disabilities if a student is going to perform at his or her potential. Common disabilities are writing disabilities (getting a thought from the brain to the pencil), reading disabilities (shifting or reversing letters or numbers occurs frequently) and visual processing problems and auditory processing problems (trouble accurately hearing what was said).

Unusual Study Habits:

Many people with ADD have unusual study habits. Most need a very quiet place to study. My wife use to go in her car under a street light to study. She needed an environment that was absolutely quiet and free from distractions. She had trouble studying at home, because she saw all the things that needed to be done and was too easily distracted. Other people with ADD need noise in order to study. Some people have told me they need the TV or radio on, or they need some noise in order to keep themselves awake and focused.

Timed Situations:

Timed testing situations are often a disaster for those with ADD. Whether it is short math "drill" exercises, classroom writing exercises or testing situations, the more time pressure that is put on these people, the worse it tends to get for them.

CHAPTER 18

The Impact Of ADD At Work

Bill, 32, had just been fired from a job he loved. He knew it was his fault, but he just couldn't organize his time to do the work that was expected. He missed deadlines, seemed to drift off in meetings, and he was often late to work. He knew that his wife would be angry with him. This was the third job he had lost in their three-year marriage. As a child, Bill had taken Ritalin for troubles in school, but he was taken off the medication when he was a teenager. His doctor told him that all kids outgrow the problems he was having. That was bad advice. At the age of 32, Bill still suffered from the effects of ADD.

When ADD is left untreated, it significantly affects the workplace. It costs employers millions of dollars every year in decreased productivity, absenteeism and employee conflicts. Yet it remains vastly underdiagnosed.

ADD can be both positive and negative in the workplace. On the positive side, people with ADD often are high in energy, enthusiastic, full of ideas, creative and they often have bursts of energy. If they surround themselves with people who organize them and manage the details, they can be very successful. In my clinical practice, I treat many highly successful ADD executives. Unfortunately, many people with ADD are not that lucky and they often have serious problems at work. Here are some of the difficulties that people with ADD are likely to have at work:

The Harder They Try, the Worse It Gets:

Research has shown that the more these people try to concentrate, the worse it gets for them. Their brain actually turns off, rather than turning on. When a supervisor or manager puts more pressure on them to perform, they often fall off in their work. The boss then interprets this decreased performance as willful misconduct and serious problems arise. I once treated a man with ADD who was a ship welder. He told me that whenever his boss put pressure on him to do a better job, his work got worse (even though he really tried to do better). When the boss told him that he liked his work, he became more productive. In supervising someone with ADD, it is much more effective to use praise and encouragement, rather than pressure.

Distractibility:

Distractibility is often evident in meetings. People with ADD tend to look around the room, drift off, appear bored, forget where the conversation is going, and interrupt with extraneous information. The distractibility and short attention span may also cause them to take much longer to complete their work than their co-workers. They are often very frustrating to managers and co-workers.

Forgetfulness:

Forgetfulness is common in ADD and a serious handicap on the job. Missed deadlines, forgotten reports and steps gone undone on a job are just a few examples.

Impulsivity:

Often, the lack of impulse control gets the ADD person fired. They may say inappropriate things to supervisors, other employees or customers. I once had a patient who was fired from 13 jobs, because he had trouble controlling his mouth. Even though he really wanted to keep several of the jobs, he would just blurt out what he was thinking before he had a chance to process the thought. Poorly thought out decisions also relate to impulsivity. Rather than thinking a problem through, these people want an immediate solution to the problem and act without the necessary forethought. In a similar vein, the impulsivity causes these people to have trouble going through the established channels at work. They often go right to the top to solve problems, rather than working through the system. This may cause resentments from their co-workers and immediate supervisors. Impulsivity also may lead to such problem behaviors as lying and stealing. I have treated many ADD people who have suffered with the shame and guilt of these behaviors.

Conflict seeking:

Many people with ADD are in constant turmoil with one or more people at work. They seem to "unconsciously" pick out people who are vulnerable and begin to pick verbal battles with them. They also have a tendency to embarrass others, which does not endear them to anyone. Shades of the grown-up version of the class clown are also evident at work, such as cracking inappropriate jokes in meetings. Conflict may follow the ADD person from job to job.

Disorganization:

Disorganization is a hallmark of ADD. Often when you look at the person's work area, it is a wonder they can work in it at all. They tend to have many piles of "stuff;" paperwork is often hard for them to keep straight; and they seem to have a filing system that only they can figure out (and only on good days).

Late to work:

Many people with ADD are chronically late to work because they have significant problems waking up in the morning. I've had several patients who bought sirens from alarm companies to help them wake up. Imagine what their neighbors thought! They also tend to lose track of time, which contributes to their lateness.

Start many projects, but finish few:

The energy and enthusiasm of people with ADD often pushes them to start many projects. Unfortunately, their distractibility and short attention span impairs their ability to complete them.

One radio station manager told me that he had started over thirty special projects the year before, but only completed a handful of them. He told me, "I'm always going to get back to them, but I get new ideas that get in the way."

I also treat a college professor who told me that the year before he saw me he started 300 different projects. His wife finished the thought by telling me he only completed three.

Moodiness and negative thinking:

Many people with ADD tend to be moody, worrisome and negative. This attitude comes from their past. They have many experiences with failure, so they come to expect it. Their "sky is falling" attitude has a tendency to get on the nerves of co-workers and can infect the work environment.

Inaccurate self-assessment:

People with ADD are often not a good judge of their own ability. They may overvalue themselves and think they are better at their jobs than they really are, or they may devalue important assets that they have.

Switches things around:

Many people with ADD have a tendency to switch things around. This happens with letters or numbers, even phrases or paragraphs. You can imagine the problems this can cause at work. Switching numbers on a phone message can cause many wrong numbers. Reading letters backwards can give different meaning to content.

Twisting information from a meeting can cause serious misunderstandings. I once treated a billing clerk who had reversed the amounts on bills she sent out, costing her employer over $12,000. I had to meet with the employer to convince him that ADD was a real phenomenon and that the employee was not trying to sabotage his business.

Tendency toward addictions:

People with ADD have a tendency toward addictions, such as food, alcohol, drugs, even work. Drug or alcohol addictions cause obvious work problems. Food addictions cause health and self-image problems which can impact work. Addiction to work is also a serious problem, because it causes burnout and family problems which eventually show up as problems at work.

Spends excessive time at work because of inefficiencies:

The symptoms of ADD frequently cause a person to be inefficient on their job. This causes many people with ADD to put in overtime that managers consider excessive. This may result in a poor job evaluation or firing. To avoid these problems, many people with ADD take their work home in order to finish it.

CHAPTER 19

The Impact Of ADD On Self-Esteen

By the age of 6 or 7, ADD often has a significant negative impact on self-esteem. Here are some of the reasons why:

Frequent Conflict:

For many, they have been in conflict with either their parents, friends or teachers over and over for years. This causes them to develop negative "self-talk" patterns and low self- esteem.

Negative Input:

The difficult behavior associated with ADD often incites negative input from others. "Don't do that. Why did you do that? Where was your head? What's wrong with you? Your brother doesn't act like that! You'd do better if you would try harder. Shame on you!" These are common phrases many ADD children hear on a regular basis. Our brains work like a computer -- negative input turns into low self-esteem.

Inaccurate self-assessment:

As mentioned above, people with ADD are often a poor judge of their own ability. They often devalue their strengths and positive attributes, focusing only on their failures.

Chronic Failure:

Most people with ADD have had many failure experiences in life, in school, relationships and work. These failures set them up to expect failure, and whenever a person expects that they will fail, they don't try their best or they don't try at all.

Negative Bonding

ADD often causes negative bonding with parents. Bonding is critical to the emotional health of human beings. Yet, by the time many ADD children are school age, they have such a negative relationship with their parents that they begin not to care about other people, which set them up for societal problems. Without bonding, people do not care about others, and when a person doesn't care, he or she has no problems hurting others to get what they want.

A Sense Of Being Damaged

Due to the many problems that ADD people have experienced throughout their lives, they often have a sense that they are different from others and that they are "damaged."

Tantrums/Rage Outbursts

As I mentioned above, there is a high incidence of rage outbursts, in people with ADD. Each outburst lowers the person's self esteem as they sense being out of control.

Brain Filters

When people do not feel good about themselves, it impairs their ability to relate to others. They have difficulty taking compliments or getting outside of themselves to truly understand the other person. The brain filters information coming in from the environment. When the brain's filter (self-esteem) is negative, people tend to only see the negative and ignore any positive. Many partners of ADD people complain that when they give their partner a compliment, they find a way to make it look like they have just been criticized.

Negative Thinking Patterns

Thought patterns are the manifestation of self-esteem. Due to difficult past life experiences, many people with ADD have a tendency to think very negatively. They frequently distort situations to make them out to be worse than they really are. They tend to mind read, overgeneralize, think in black or white terms, predict bad outcomes, label themselves with negative terms and personalize situations that have little meaning. Teaching the ADD person to talk back to negative thoughts is essential to helping them heal.

POINTS TO REMEMBER

**ADD is a neurobiological disorder with
serious psychological and social consequences.**

**Children, teens, adults
and parents need to know:**

**It's not their fault,
they didn't cause it,
and there is a lot of hope.**

**Parents, spouses and family members
need information and**

**the child, teenager or adult
needs good treatment.**

PART IV

TREATMENT AND EFFECTIVE LIVING WITH ADD

CHAPTER 20

Components Of Treatment For ADD

Treatment for ADD must be multi-dimensional if it's to be the most effective. Medication by itself is not nearly as effective as combining it with the other treatments listed below.

1. Superior Parenting Skills

2. Effective Behavior Shaping and Modifying Techniques

3. Family Effectiveness Strategies

4. Social Skills Work

5. Classroom Management and Homework Strategies

6. Brain Wave Biofeedback

7. Goal-Directed Psychotherapy Techniques

8. Specific Treatment Tips For Adults

9. Medication

10. Proper Sleep Management Techniques

11. Emotional Reprogramming

12. Understanding The Legal Rights Of People With ADD

CHAPTER 21

Superior Parenting Skills

Even those with the best parenting skills deteriorate when they're up against the day-to-day stress of ADD kids. Work with the parents and family is crucial to a healthy outcome for these children. Having an ADD child is often extremely stressful on a family system. Siblings are often embarrassed by the child's behavior, and parents often feel guilty for not liking these children very much. One of the most helpful things I do for these children is to lead a weekly parent education and support group. When I help parents become more effective with these children, the entire household does better.

Before undertaking parent training, it is important to screen parents for ADD. Untreated ADD in parents sabotages treatment, because parents are often unable to follow through on their homework.

Here is a summary of the important points from the course:

1. Be focused. Set clear goals for yourself as a parent and for your child. Then make sure that you act in a way that is consistent with your goals.

2. Relationship is key. With a good parent-child relationship almost any form of discipline will work. With a poor parent-child relationship, any form of discipline will probably fail.

Relationships require two things:

time

and

a willingness to listen.

3. Spend some "special time" with your child each day, even if it's only 10 to 15 minutes. Being available to the child will help him or her feel important and enhance his or her self esteem.

4. Be a good listener. Find out what the child thinks before you tell him or her what you think.

5. Be clear with what you expect. It is effective for families to have posted rules, spelling out the "laws" and values of the family. For example, "We treat each other with respect, which means no yelling, no hitting, no name calling or putdowns. We look for ways to make each other's lives easier."

6. When a child lives up to the rules and expectations, be sure to notice him or her. If you never reinforce good behavior, you're unlikely to get much of it.

7. Notice the behaviors you like in your child 10 times more than the behaviors you don't like. This teaches them to notice what they like about themselves rather than to grow up with a critical self-image.

8. Mean what you say. Don't allow guilt to cause you to back down on what you know is right.

9. Don't tell a child 10 times to do something. Expect a child to comply the first time! Be ready to back up your words.

10. Never discipline a child when you're out of control. Take a time out before you lose your cool.

11. Use discipline to teach a child rather than to punish or get even for bad behavior.

12. See misbehavior as a problem you're going to solve rather than "the child is just trying to make you mad."

13. It's important to have swift, clear consequences for broken rules, enforced in a "matter of fact" and unemotional way. Nagging and yelling are extremely destructive, ineffective and tend to be addictive for the ADD child.

14. Give a child choices between alternatives, rather than dictating what they'll do, eat or wear. If you make all the decisions for your child, he or she will be unable to make their own decisions later on.

15. Parents need to be together and support each other. When children are allowed to split parental authority, they have far more power than is good for them.

16. Keep promises to children.

17. Children learn about relationships from watching how their parents relate to each other. Are you setting a good example?

18. Children live up to the labels we give them. Be careful of the nicknames and phrases you use to describe your children.

19. Parents need time for themselves. Parents who are drained do not have much left that is good for their children.

20. Teach children from your own real life experiences.

21. In parenting, always remember the words "firm and kind." One parent used the phrase, "tough as nails and kind as a lamb." Try to balance them at the same time.

GET RID OF GUILT

Perhaps the biggest roadblock to effective discipline of ADD children and teens is GUILT. Too often parents allow guilt to get in their way and render them totally ineffective in dealing with the difficult child.

Here is the **GUILT CYCLE** that often perpetuates bad behavior.

PARENT EXPLODES
(because they can't take the bad behavior any more)

PARENT FEELS GUILT
(because they overreacted or were excessively harsh)

**PARENT ALLOWS THE CHILD TO
GET AWAY WITH MISBEHAVIOR**
(because of their guilt over the explosion toward the child)

PARENT FEELS TENSION BUILDING UP
(because they are not effectively dealing with the misbehavior)

PARENT EXPLODES
(and the cycle starts all over again)

It's very important when dealing with the ADD child to break the guilt cycle. The best way to do this is by dealing with difficult behavior whenever it occurs and not allowing the tension to build up in you to the point where you explode.

Thoughts On Television and Video Games

In our mobile society, with a lack of extended family support and where both parents usually work outside the home, parents have needed to find prolonged daycare and baby-sitter situations for their children. This is particularly true for difficult children, who often go through day care providers, as they go through pairs of shoes. Many families in our society have found the answer to their baby-sitting problems: television and video games.

The amount of time that children and teenagers (and even adults) spend watching television and playing video games has more than doubled over the past 30 years. On average, children spend much less time playing with friends and much more time playing with remote controls, joysticks and keyboards. There are several reasons why this trend is harmful to children, especially children and teens with ADD.

First, extended time watching television or playing video games takes time away from social interactions. Children need social interactions in order to mature and to be able to relate to others as adults. Children who have difficulty in social situations are often happy to escape the painful interactions with others. Thus, they are less likely to learn the social skills they need to get along.

Second, watching television and playing video games are often passive, "no brain" activities. With television, everything is provided for the viewer, nothing is left to the imagination. The mind is a passive recipient of the action on the tube. Video games are only slightly different. Whenever a person plays a new game, they need to figure out strategy and use thinking skills to beat the game. That part is good. But most children and teens who play these games, do so on a repetitive basis. They play the same game, over and over and over. Thus, like television, it becomes a "no brain" activity. In EEG or brain wave studies that I have performed in my office, both television and video games are a "no brain" activity. These activities do not activate a person's brain; rather they cause a decrease in brain activity. The brain is like a muscle, the more that it is used, the stronger it becomes. The more time that it spends in passive activities, the weaker it becomes. There have been other studies in the past several years that have demonstrated that achievement and performance in school are inversely related to the amount of time spent watching television or playing video games. The more TV or video games, the worse the grades and performance scores in school.

Three, television and video games are not an appropriate place to learn values and problem-solving skills. With the fast pace of society and the overall decline of religious values in the every -day lives of children and teens, television (and yes, even video games) has become a prime source of programming values.

Typical television values and messages include:

when you're angry, you can hit or shoot someone
 (violence is a very common way people solve problems on television),

the good life is depicted with lite beer and skinny women
 (encouraging alcohol abuse and eating disorders)

sexual promiscuity
 (as seen in three o'clock in the afternoon on MTV)

being sarcastic and rude is funny and acceptable family behavior
 (from All In The Family to The Simpsons and Married With Children)
 and

the world is a dangerous place to live
 (anyone who watches the evening news knows this).

Here are several family rules for watching television and playing video games to consider:

* limit the time per day of both television and video games
   (no more than an hour total)

* supervise what they watch and the games they play

* discuss television scenes that impact on a child or teen's morals and values

* encourage more creative and productive activities for children and teens, where they use their minds.

CHAPTER 22

Effective Behavior Shaping and Modifying Techniques

Retraining difficult behavior patterns is an essential part of the treatment for ADD. As I've mentioned, having this disorder causes faulty learning in many areas of life. For example, many children with ADD are repeatedly given the message that they're stupid (i.e., by parent or teacher complaints, being teased by other children). Their mind begins to believe they really are stupid. As such, they stop doing their work, believing it is too hard for them.

Behaviorally, many children, teens and adults learn to get other people upset with their difficult behavior. They learn, on a purely unconscious and biological level, that when there is turmoil between people, it stimulates their brain, making them feel more alert and awake. They do not know this on a conscious level and would, in fact, deny that they ever do it. But, when you watch these people with their parents or in social situations, their behavior seems goal directed toward turmoil. After listening to hundreds of mothers, I'm convinced that these people are treating their underlying brain deactivation with turmoil, like an alcoholic may treat underlying restlessness or anxiety with booze.

Retraining behavior patterns or behavior modification involves several clear steps:

STEPS TO CHANGING/SHAPING BEHAVIOR

Step One:

> **Specifically define the desired and
> undesirable behaviors.**

Step Two:

> **Establish a baseline period**

Step Three:

> **Clearly communicate the rules and expectations.**

Step Four:

> **Reward desired behavior.**

Step Five:

> **Clear, unemotional consequences
> for the negative behavior.**

Step One:

Specifically define the desired and undesirable behaviors. Before you can shape behavior, it is critical to clearly know what behaviors you want and what behaviors you don't want. Examples of desirable behaviors might include doing what parents say the first time or doing homework before going out to play. Hitting another person and talking back are examples of undesirable behaviors.

Step Two:

Establish a baseline period of how often either negative or positive behavior occurs. Take some time (a week to a month) to keep a log on how many times a behavior occurs. For example, if the desired behavior is getting homework done before a child or teen goes out of the house, keep a log on how many times that actually occurs during the baseline period. Doing this will allow you to know whether or not your interventions are effective.

Step Three:

Clearly communicate rules and expectations. Establishing clear, written rules and expectations is the next step in effective behavior modification. These rules need to give direction for the child's behavior. When they know what is expected, they are much more likely to be able to give it. Too often, parents believe that children should know how to act without the rules being clearly communicated to them.

Another reason to have the rules written is that children respond to symbols of rules in the environment (traffic signals, posted rules at the pool, etc.) As opposed to the 55 mile per hour speed limit, children are often rule-oriented and respond to signs. My nephew Andrew went through a time when he was three years old where he was afraid of monsters in his room at night. Week after week, Andrew's parents searched the room with Andrew, trying to prove to him that there were no monsters in his room. They looked under the bed, in the closet, behind the door and under the covers. Finally, they realized that they were only making the fear worse by exploring the room for the monsters. Andrew's mother decided that they would make a sign saying that monsters were not allowed in Andrew's room. She and Andrew drew a picture of a monster and then drew a red circle around it with a slash across the monster. Underneath the picture they wrote "NO MONSTERS ALLOWED." Amazingly, Andrew's fear of monsters in his room vanished because he knew the sign kept them away.

Written rules have power! They let children know what is expected of them in a clear way. They allow you to know when the children are following the rules and they give you a basis for reinforcing them. They also clearly allow you to know when they are not following the rules and serve as a touch point for clear, unemotional consequences.

Here is a set of rules that I've found helpful (both for my own household and for my patients'). Post them up where the family can see them every day.

FAMILY RULES

TELL THE TRUTH

TREAT EACH OTHER WITH RESPECT
(which means no yelling, no hitting, no kicking,
no name calling, and no putting down)

NO ARGUING WITH PARENTS
(as parents, we want and value your input and ideas,
but arguing means you have made your point more than one time)

RESPECT EACH OTHER'S PROPERTY
(which means we ask permission to use
something that does not belong to us

DO WHAT MOM AND DAD
SAY THE FIRST TIME
(without complaining or throwing a fit)

ASK PERMISSION BEFORE
YOU GO SOMEWHERE

PUT THINGS AWAY
THAT YOU TAKE OUT

LOOK FOR WAYS TO BE KIND
AND HELPFUL TO EACH OTHER

These rules set the tone and "values" for the family. They clearly state that there is a line of authority at home, and that it is expected that children will follow the rules and respect their parents, their siblings and the family's property. These are good social expectations and teachings. When you tell someone what you expect, you're much more likely to get it.

In establishing expectations at home, it's often important to use visual clues, such as pictures or short printed directions. Try to minimize verbal directions since people with ADD may have trouble processing verbal input (especially in a noisy environment). Writing expectations down also has the advantage of being able to refer to it later when the ADD person denies that you ever told him about it.

Step Four:

Reward desired behavior. After clear expectations are given, it is essential to praise and reward the behavior that meets those expectations. When positive behavior goes unnoticed, it often ceases to exist. Most children, teens and even adults enjoy being noticed by others. Rewards or reinforcers may take many forms. As adults, we often work for monetary gain. The more financial benefit, the harder we'll work. But we also work for praise from our boss or spouse. Our personalities often determine the rewards we're interested in working toward. Children are the same way -- some children will work hard to comply for the verbal praise of their parents, while others need different types of rewards. Here is a list of different reinforcers.

Social rewards: verbal praise, "I really like it when you...." physical affection, such as hugs or looks.

Material rewards: toys, food, "clean your room before your snack," little presents or surprises.

Activity rewards: sports, trips to library, park, arcade.

Token rewards: star or point systems, money.

Here are some simple principles in rewarding good behavior:

** use many more rewards than punishment,

** reward as soon as possible after a child fulfills your expectations,

** focus your energy on catching them being good,

** look for ways to reinforce them,

** reward the child in a way he or she likes
   (all children are different; use what works!),

** be consistent,

** make it to the child's benefit to behave.

Many parents object to the use of reward systems when it comes to reinforcing good behavior. They say, "I'm not going to bribe my child to behave. They should do it anyway." I respond that the definition of a bribe is to give someone something of value to encourage them to do something illegal. Behaving is not illegal! Generally, adults would not go to work if there was not some sort of payoff. It is important to think that children also work for goals and payoffs that turn them on. For difficult kids, it is often necessary to set up a token system or a point system to help keep them on track.

Here is a simple five-step "point" or "chip" system that has worked well for hundreds of parents.

1. Choose

-- three chores (such as doing the dishes, cleaning their room, vacuuming, feeding the animals, etc.) and

-- three behaviors (such as treating their sister well, getting ready for school on time, doing what mom and dad say the first time, etc.).

2. Assign a point (or poker chip) value to each chore and behavior depending on how difficult each is for the child to accomplish. If the child has a lot of trouble doing something, make it worth more points or chips than something

he can do easily. Add up the possible points or chips the child can get each day if he or she has a perfect day. Also, let the child know that he or she can earn bonus points or chips for especially cooperative and pleasant behavior. Tell the child that points or chips will only be given for chores and behaviors done on the first request. If you have to repeat yourself, the child will not get any points or chips.

3. Establish two lists of rewards:

-- one for future incentives the child wishes to work for (toy, having a friend spend the night, special trip to restaurant or arcade, renting a video, etc.),

-- another list for everyday rewards (watching TV, playing with friends, playing video games, staying up an extra half hour, etc.).

4. Determine the point value necessary to redeem each reward. About half should be spent on every day rewards. This allows a child, if they have a really good day, to save about half of their points or chips for special rewards down the line.

5. Everyday add up the points and allow the child to use his or her rewards to buy everyday privileges and keep a "savings account" for them for the points or chips they are able to save up to be used later on. This works to teach them the value and need for saving.

Note:

** Initially, make the system very reinforcing so that children will want to participate. Then slowly tighten the reins on it as their behavior improves.

** You can use the rewards for almost any behavior you like.

** Reward as quickly as possible.

** Do not give chips or points away before the actual behavior or chore is done. In this system, there is no credit!

Fat Freddy's Mode Of Changing Behavior

I'm a little embarrassed to tell you that I collect penguins. I now have over 400 penguins in my office. They remind me of the need to shape behavior in a positive way. I used to live in Hawaii. On the island of Oahu, there is a place by the name of Sea Life Park, which is like Marine World and Sea World with sea animal shows. At Sea Life Park they had a penguin show, and the penguin's name was Fat Freddy. Freddy could do amazing things, clearly amazing things. He could jump off a 20-foot board, he could bowl with his nose, he could count, he even jumped through a hoop of fire. I was really taken with this penguin. I watched Freddy's show with my son, Antony, who was seven at the time.

Toward the end of the show the trainer asked Freddy to go get something and Freddy went and got it and brought it right back. I was really taken back in my mind when I saw this. I thought to myself, "I ask this kid to get me something and he wants to have a discussion with me for 20 minutes and then he doesn't want to do it. What's the difference? I know my son is smarter than this penguin." Anyway, we went up to the trainer after the show and I asked her how she got Freddy to do all of those really neat things. The trainer looked at my son and then she looked at me and she said "Unlike parents, whenever Freddy does anything like what I want him to do, I notice him, I give him a hug and then I give him a fish."

Even though my son doesn't like fish, the light really turned on in my head: whenever he did things that I liked, I paid no attention to him at all because I'm a very busy guy. But whenever he did something I didn't like, I gave him a ton of attention because I don't want to raise bad kids. Well guess what I was doing -- I was encouraging him to be a pain in the neck -- and in that way get noticed more and more by me.

So I collect penguins as a way to remind myself to notice the good things about the people in my life a lot more than the bad things about them. This is the essence of shaping behavior.

Step Five:

Clear, unemotional consequences for the negative behavior. In order for consequences to be effective, they must be used with the other steps in shaping behavior, i.e., clear expectations, positive reinforcement. Consequences by themselves change nothing, but when used in conjunction with the other steps of the program they can be very powerful in helping to parent the difficult child.

I once saw an interaction between a mother and her 4-year-old son in a grocery store that turned my stomach. After the child ran off for the third time, the mother jerked him by the arm, picked him off the ground and whacked him so hard his little body flew into the air. She then slammed him down into the cart and said, "You little brat, do what I say!" With a panicked look, he held his little arms up to hug her, at which point she turned and looked away from him. He then started to cry.

Too often parents punish children as a reaction to the anger they feel inside and when they're out of control of themselves. This type of punishment causes the child to feel frightened and angry and the parent to feel guilty and frustrated.

It's important to distinguish between punishment and discipline. Punishment means to inflict a penalty for wrong doing. Discipline, from the root word disciple, means to teach or train. It's critical that we use discipline to teach children how to be good, rather than inflict punishment when they're not.

As I mentioned above, reinforcing good behavior is a much more effective change agent than giving consequences to bad behavior. Yet, there still are times when consequences are needed.

Here are eight components of effective discipline:

1. A good relationship with a child is a prerequisite to effective discipline. When parents have a good relationship with a child, almost any form of discipline is effective. When the relationship is poor, however, almost no form of discipline works well. Never discipline children in a way that damages your relationship with them.

2. You must be in control of yourself. If you feel like you're going to explode, take a time out: take several deep breaths, count to fifty, hit a pillow, take a walk, call a friend, do anything to avoid exploding at the child. It's impossible to discipline effectively when you're out of control, and it does more harm than good.

3. DON'T YELL, NAG OR BELITTLE. What happens inside you when someone yells, nags or belittles you? If you're like me you immediately turn them off. These are very ineffective, and harm the relationship more than help the situation. Also, remember in Chapter One I wrote that there are some kids who get unconsciously "turned on" by turmoil. When you feel like yelling, talk softly (the difference in your behavior will frighten them).

4. Have a goal in mind for the behavior you're trying to change. For the mother above, the goal was to get the child to stay near her. She would be more effective if she gave him a lot of positive attention for the time he stays near her, rather than giving him a lot of negative attention for when he goes away. By thinking in a positive way about the behaviors you'd like the child to change, you're more likely to be helpful to him or her.

5. Develop a plan for discipline before you're actually in the situation. This also prevents you from overreacting. Discipline should be as immediate as possible and should be a reminder to the child on how to change his or her behavior, not an assault. I often recommend a short time out method for younger children and a little bit longer one for older children. Parents can also have their children write lines or essays on how they'll change their behavior.

6. Whenever possible, use NATURAL and LOGICAL consequences. Ask yourself, "What's the natural or logical consequence to the misbehavior?" If the child refuses to do his homework, then he goes to school without it. If it is acting up at dinner so that he is put in a time out for 10 minutes, then he doesn't get to finish dinner if everyone else is done. If she refuses to put away her toys, then it is logical that they will be taken away for several days. Using these natural or logical consequences help children learn cause and effect and teaches them that they are responsible for their behavior.

7. Attitude is everything. Many parents ask my opinion on spanking. I generally tell them that whether or not you spank a child has nothing to do with effective discipline. How you discipline, not the method, is what's important.

When you mildly spank a child when you're in control of yourself, for a specific reason, on the buttocks, and afterwards give the child a hug, then spanking can be very effective. However, most parents don't use it that way. They spank a child when they're angry and on the verge of being out of control themselves. Use discipline for teaching. You and your child will both feel better.

8. Never withhold love, affection or time from a child who has misbehaved. When children are in trouble, they need you the most. Let them know it's their behavior you're disciplining, but you still love them very much.

A TIME OUT METHOD THAT WORKS

When used properly, TIME OUT is an extremely effective discipline technique for children 2 to 12 years of age. Use following guidelines:

1. Give clear commands. For example, "Antony, take out the trash now." And then count to 5 or ten seconds to yourself. If you count out loud you teach the child to cue off your voice.

2. Expect immediate compliance. We teach our kids when to respond to us. When we repeat ourselves ten times and then get serious with a child, we're teaching them not to listen to us until the tenth time we say something. Expect your child to obey you the first time you say something. When they do comply, notice and appreciate them. In our example, "Thanks Antony, I really like it when you do what I say the first time."

3. When the child doesn't comply, warn them only once and give them the choice to comply. In our case, "Antony, I told you to take out the trash now (spoken in a firm, but not hostile tone). You have a choice. You can take it out now or you can spend 10 minutes in time out and then you can do it. It's up to you."

4. If the child still doesn't comply IMMEDIATELY, put him or her in TIME OUT!

5. TIME OUTs are best served in a neutral, boring corner of the house. Don't use the child's bedroom because you have probably gone to great lengths and expense to make their bedroom a nice place to be. Use a TIME OUT chair, be-

cause there may be times when the child has to be in it for a while. Also, with a chair you can set the rule that in order for them to be in TIME OUT both of their buttocks need to be on the seat of the chair.

6. The time in TIME OUT should be their age in minutes or twice their age in minutes for more severe offenses. For example, if the child is 5 years old the TIME OUT should be five minutes long (or ten minutes if it was a particularly bad offense). It's often good to get a timer to clearly set the time.

7. Their time starts when they are quiet. Children should not be allowed to badger you when they are in TIME OUT. It is a time for them to think about their behavior and they can't think about it when their mouths are going! If they start to cry, whine or nag you, simply reset the timer. Say very little; difficult kids may try to engage you in a fight but don't take the bait.

8. Don't give in to their protests about being in TIME OUT. The first few times you use this method, your child may become extremely upset. Expect it. But KNOW you're going to follow through! In unusual situations, children may cry, fight or whine for several hours. They believe if they irritate you enough, then you'll give in to their tantrum. Whatever you do, do your best to hang in there and not give in to the tantrum. Simply repeat to them, "Your time starts when you are quiet," and nothing else. If you go for 2 hours the first time and hold firm, it's likely the next time will be only an hour, then a half hour, then pretty soon the child will go to TIME OUT without a fuss. The first time you use TIME OUT, don't do it when you're in a hurry to go somewhere. Be sure to leave yourself enough time to be able to do it right.

9. If the child refuses to stay in TIME OUT you have several choices.

   -- You can tell the child that he or she will get two spankings on their buttocks if they get out (make sure you're in control of yourself before you use this method).

   -- You can take away points or chips if they are on a token system.

   -- You can ground them from activities they enjoy.

10. In order for the child to get out of TIME OUT, he or she must promise to do the thing they were asked to do and apologize for not doing it the first time they

were asked. If they refuse to do it, they remain in TIME OUT until they do. It's very important to give the child the message that you're SERIOUS and that you MEAN what you say! If they can't do it or they broke a rule such as "no hitting" they must promise not to do it again. The apology they give you must be sincere. It's important that we teach children the value of "conscience" and feeling sorry when they do things that are wrong.

11. If the child has siblings who bother or tease them when they're in TIME OUT, make the sibling take their place. This is a very effective technique in keeping the others kids from further inflaming the situation.

For teenagers, it is more effective and less humiliating to use "response cost" methods. When they break a rule or fail to comply that negative "response" costs them something important to them, such as privileges, money, phone time, going out on the weekends, etc. Make sure the consequence fits the crime. I've treated some teenagers who were grounded for the summer. By July they became depressed.

Make discipline

a time for teaching

and reshaping behavior.

CHAPTER 23

Family Effectiveness Strategies

Families often fall victim to undiagnosed or untreated ADD. Involving the whole family in treatment is often essential for a healthy outcome. Here are some important family treatment issues to consider.

Screen Other Family Members For ADD:

ADD usually has genetic underpinnings. When one member has ADD, it is more likely that another person may have it as well. Trying to effectively treat a family when one or more members have an untreated case of ADD is inviting frustration and failure. It is helpful to do some screening on every member of the immediate family. I have found that when parents have un-treated ADD, they have trouble following through on medication schedules for their children or the parent training suggestions given as part of therapy. When a sibling goes undiagnosed, he or she often sabotages the process by their conflict-seeking behavior.

Communication Issues

Families with one or more persons with ADD often have serious com-munication issues. There is a tendency to misinterpret information, react pre-maturely or have emotional outbursts over real or imagined slights. It is essential to teach families how to listen, clarify misunderstandings and avoid mind reading. It is also essential to teach families with one or more ADD members to communicate in a clear, unemotional manner. Emotionality de-creases effectiveness in communication.

Calm The Drive Toward Turmoil:

As I've mentioned many times now, ADD children, teenagers and adults are often experts at getting others to yell at them. It is essential, therefore, to teach families how to calm volatile situations. Teaching simple breathing techniques to all family members can be very valuable in calming disagreements. Also, the use of family time outs can be helpful when a situation starts to escalate. In family time outs, everyone in the family goes to a quiet part of the house for a designated period of time (10 -15 minutes), whenever voices are raised or someone is losing control. Of course, family time outs need to be set up ahead of time if they are going to work in calming difficult situations.

Get Rid Of Guilt:

Guilt is an issue for many in an ADD family. Resentment, bad feelings and anger are common in family members, yet these feelings are foreign and uncomfortable. Parents, spouses or siblings feel that they are not "supposed" to have bad feelings toward people they love, and they end up burdened by feelings of guilt. It is essential to teach family members that these resentments are normal given the difficulties in the family. Explaining the biological nature of ADD to family members often helps them understand the turmoil and have more compassion toward the person with ADD, while alleviating any guilt they might feel.

Dealing With Embarrassment

Embarrassment is a common feeling in ADD family members. The outrageous behavior and public displays of turmoil often lead family members to want to hide from the outside world. Siblings complain that their friends tease them at school because of their brother or sister's behavior, parents are frequently subjected to disapproving looks from store clerks or other parents who have "perfect" kids. Again, helping families understand ADD will help them deal with the embarrassment.

Good Guy Versus Bad Guy

In families with ADD, people often get a "good guy versus bad guy" label. Children with the disorder often find that their behavior causes them to be outcasts or "black sheep." Whenever there is trouble, parents, unconsciously, look to them first. This "good guy versus bad guy" phenomena also applies to parents. A parent who has ADD, often gets labeled by the other parent as emotional, irrational or troubled. By doing this, the ADD parent may be stripped of his or her authority, causing resentment and turmoil. Treating the disorder in all family members who have it, along with teaching the family to share power is essential to treating this "good guy versus bad guy" phenomena.

Split Families

Divorce is more common in ADD families. This may be due to many factors, such as the increased turmoil caused by ADD children or the interpersonal problems of the ADD adults. Thus, the issues of divorce, custody and step families need to be addressed in treatment.

No question, I've seen a higher percentage of families with ADD children break up through divorce. This is due, in large part, to the turmoil caused by these children. Parents often blame each other for the problems and begin to pull apart. For parents who work, who wants to work all day and then come home to a house filled with tension? For parents who stay home, who wants to be in a battle zone all day and then have a spouse come home who doesn't want to hear about all of the problems of the day? After a while, people get burned out and they may look elsewhere for some satisfaction in their lives. This dynamic may make them more vulnerable to becoming workaholics or having extramarital affairs.

Because of the higher divorce rate, child custody often becomes an issue. I do many child custody evaluations in my practice. I look for the parent who is best suited to help the child have a good relationship with both parents, rather than a parent who vilifies the other one.

Step family issues are also very important for many of these families. All members of the families need to be educated about ADD, including its effects on families and the treatment. Also, encouraging a positive attitude and open communication between families is essential to having a healthy situation. With the ADD person's drive toward turmoil, the child or adult may unconsciously seek conflict, and step families are often more vulnerable to misunderstandings and tension.

What To Do About Dad

Unfortunately, men are often the last people to admit that there are emotional or family problems. They often delay treatment, for their children or themselves, until there has been a negative effect on self-esteem or functioning. I have heard many men tell me that there is nothing wrong with their son, even though he may have been expelled from school on numerous occasions 3 years in a row. "He is just like I was when I was young and I turned out OK," they say.

Why men are less likely to see emotional or family problems is the subject of much debate. Here are some possibilities:

** many men have trouble verbalizing their feelings,

** many men have difficulty getting outside of themselves to see the needs of others,

** men tend to be more action oriented than women,

** societal expectations seem to be that men can handle problems on their own and they are weak if they seek help,

** men aren't allowed to cry, or express any negative feelings, so they never learn to seek help or talk through their problems.

Whatever the reason, men in ADD families need education about ADD and they need to be part of the treatment process if it is to have the best chance of being successful. To this end, it is important for wives, mothers and the therapist to engage the father in a positive way and encourage him to see his valuable role in helping the whole family heal. ADD is a family problem and needs the support of everyone to be successful.

Living With A Partner With ADD

When one or both partners in a marriage (or other living situation) has ADD, it is important understand the couple dynamics and the treatment process. Here are important issues to consider:

-- Have empathy for the ADD person and try to see the world through their eyes of frustration and failure

-- Go to at least some appointments with the doctor together. When I treat adults with ADD, I prefer to see both partners together, at least some of the time, to gather another perspective on the treatment progress. I'm often amazed at the different perspective I get from a person's partner.

-- Both partners need clear education on ADD, its genetic roots, how it impacts couples, and its treatment.

-- After the initial diagnosis, take a step back from the chronic turmoil that may have been present in the relationship. Look at your relationship from a new perspective and, if need be, try to start over.

-- Set up regular time for talking and checking in.

-- Keep lists to avoid resentments for chores and tasks not done.

-- Assume the best about the other person.

-- Set clear goals for each area of your life together and review them on a regular basis. Evaluate whether your behavior is getting you what you want. For example, I want a kind, caring, loving and supportive relationship with my wife. But, sometimes her behavior irritates me beyond belief. I can impulsively respond in an angry way (which has never been helpful) or I can choose to respond in a loving, helpful way which more closely matches my goals with her. When you know what you want, you are much more able to make it happen.

-- Set clear individual goals and share them with each other. Then look for ways to help the other person reach their personal goals.

-- Avoid stereotyped roles of "caretaker" and "sick one."

-- Talk out issues concerning sex, in a kind and caring manner.

-- Frequently check in with each other during social gatherings, to see the comfort level of each partner.

-- Get away, alone together on a regular basis. This is especially important when there are ADD kids in the family.

-- Work together in parenting children. Children with ADD put a tremendous strain on relationships. This is magnified even further when one of the parents has ADD as well. See yourselves as partners, not adversaries.

-- Praise each other ten times more than you criticize!

-- Get rid of the smelly bucket of fish (hurts from the past) that you carry around. Many couples hold on to old hurts and use them to torture each other months to years later. These "smelly fish" are destructive and stink up a relationship. Clean them out of your life.

-- If the ADD person refuses to get help, even after repeated encouragement to do so, the partner must consider whether or not to stay in the relationship. Many people with ADD have such a wounded sense of themselves that they refuse to acknowledge any problems, and refuse to accept any help or treatment. At this point, the spouse or lover should not protect or cover for the ADD person, since this only makes them more dependent and less likely to seek help. In fact, I have seen many occasions where the spouse's leaving the relationship led the ADD person into treatment for themselves. Co-dependency is not just a term for spouses of alcoholics, it applies to those who protect and help adults with ADD, thus preventing them from having to be grown up on their own.

CHAPTER 24

Help In Getting Along With Others

Making and keeping friends is difficult for many people with ADD. It is estimated that at least half of all children and teens with ADD have problems with their peers and up to 75% of adults have interpersonal problems. In treating people with ADD of all ages, it is often important to include a social skills component to the treatment.

Here are several of the reasons for social problems:

** a high rate of intrusive or disruptive behaviors (excessive talking, interrupting, noisy and obnoxious behavior, monopolizing discussions)

** limited social reciprocity (problems taking turns and sharing, difficulty following others in conversations, poor eye contact, inappropriate verbal interchanges)

** poor emotional control (excitability, moodiness, temper outbursts, overreaction to minor events)

** impulsivity (saying or doing things that are thoughtless)

** distractibility (trouble focusing on others)

** lack of follow through (makes relationships feel one-sided from the other person's point of view)

The components of effective social skills treatment often need to include:

** teaching communication skills, including active listening (repeating back the information and feelings you hear before you respond)

** providing an environment for successful peer contacts and positive experiences (encourage the ADD person to invite peers over to the house to spend time together)

** increase knowledge about appropriate behavior (look for situations to teach the child about helpful social behavior; discussing interactions that are seen on TV or in stores can be very helpful)

** teach self-monitoring and internal dialogue techniques (these include techniques that teach people to question what they do before they do it, to stop and think through the consequences to their behavior before they act in a certain way)

** search for areas of social competence (sports, karate, music) and give the ADD person healthy doses of these activities

** diligently work on decreasing aggressive behavior at home and school; aggressiveness is one of the strongest predictors of peer rejection

A good place to start social skill training is with the siblings at home. I believe it is essential to expect siblings to be civil and act appropriately toward each other. Many psychologists say "let the children work out their own problems, don't interfere." I disagree with this notion. Remember what happened to Cain and Abel when their parents didn't intervene? In sibling relationships, clearly state that you expect them to treat each other with respect. When they are positive and appropriate with each other, notice and praise them. When they are inappropriate, condescending, aggressive or mean with each other, discipline them. When parents lay out the ground rules, siblings are much more likely to get along with each other, which may translate to them behaving more appropriately with others.

CHAPTER 25

Classroom And Homework Management Strategies

Finding the best classroom and homework strategies are critical to school success for people with ADD. Here are the strategies I give my patients:

The Teacher

-- the teacher is a major determining factor on how well the child or teen will do in school. Choose carefully!

-- look for a teacher who understands ADD or is at least willing to learn about it,

-- look for a teacher who will keep in regular contact with you about your child's progress,

-- look for a teacher who protects the child or teen's self-esteem and will not put him down in front of other children or allow other children to make fun of him. Singling out a child sets him or her up to be to be teased by their peers!

-- look for a teacher who has clear and consistent rules, so that the child or teen knows what to expect,

-- look for a teacher who cannot be manipulated easily and who is firm, yet kind,

-- look for a teacher who will motivate and encourage,

-- look for a teacher who realizes the tremendous effort these children and teenagers need to put out in order to be average,

-- look for a teacher who has an exciting and stimulating presentation style, using multi-sensory teaching methods (visual, auditory and kinesthetic),

-- look for a teacher who gives directions slowly and clearly, and is willing to repeat them if necessary and check to see if the ADD child or teen is following them correctly

-- look for a teacher who will make adaptations as necessary, such as decrease the amount of an assignment, allow more time for tasks, allow for the use of calculators, etc.,

-- look for a teacher who will not undermine the treatment you have with your doctor. I've known some uninformed teachers who had the nerve to tell parents, "I'm really opposed to medication."

I realize that "no teacher" possesses all of these traits, but look for teachers who have an open mind and know or are willing to learn about ADD. Having a helpful, positive teacher is often the difference between success and failure for the person with ADD.

Environment

-- do not cover every wall with art work, posters and pictures; visually stimulating material may distract ADD students,

-- the person may need to leave the class for mastering concepts or resource assistance,

-- usually it is best to seat the child up front, near the teacher with his or her back to the rest of the students to decrease distractions,

-- reduce or minimize distractions (both audio and visual); do not place an ADD student near the air conditioner, heater, high traffic areas, doors or windows,

-- make earphones available to allow children to decrease auditory distractions,

-- cooling off periods when upset,

-- decrease highly stimulating things in the environment,

-- use of written, displayed rules,

-- surround ADD students with "good role models,"

-- encourage cooperative and collaborative learning,

-- help the ADD student feel comfortable seeking help. Many of these students won't ask questions for fear of appearing stupid to their peers,

-- most fights and "acting out" behavior at school occurs in the cafeteria because of the noise and confusion. Providing a quiet place for lunch may decrease the number of lunch time problems for these children,

-- ADD children often come in from recess or lunch "wound up." Have the entire class walk around the room, then pretend to be palm trees swaying in the breeze. "How slowly can you sway?" is a calming down exercise that will help start the late morning or afternoon session off right,

-- if lines are a problem for the child, place him or her at the end of the line where people will not be brushing up against their body; these kids are very sensitive to touch.

Pacing

-- adjust time for completion of projects,

-- allow frequent breaks, vary activity often,

-- omit assignments requiring copying in a timed situation,

-- give only one assignment at a time.

Increasing Attentiveness

-- pause after a question and look at different students before calling on anyone to answer,

-- alert students that you are going to ask a question (e.g., "I am going to call on someone soon - I don't know who yet."),

-- encourage students to look at the student who is answering,

-- create a level of uncertainly that requires more than passive receptivity (e.g., "What do you think will happen next?"),

-- if a teacher sees a student's attention wandering, call his name and ask a simple question he can answer,

-- use "attention recording sheets" for self-monitoring; student marks a plus each time he realizes he has been paying attention and a minus each time he realizes his mind has wandered,

-- have students record time taken to complete tasks (e.g., note starting time at the top of the page and ending time at the bottom -- actual time is not important, but the process of self-monitoring is crucial). A watch with a stop watch and an alarm can be very helpful for these children and teens,

-- have students grade their own papers and tests. This reinforces a habit of reviewing their own work,

-- use nonverbal or secret cues to keep the child on track.

Presentation of Subject Matter

-- emphasize teaching approach according to learning style of student (audio/visual/tactile/multi),

-- vibrant, enthusiastic teachers,

-- increased class participation in lectures,

-- highly interactive, interesting, novel and stimulating,

-- individual or small group discussions,

-- taped lectures for replay,

-- use demonstrations to illustrate points,

-- utilize "hands on" activities,

-- emphasize critical information, teach the BIG PICTURE,

-- new concepts and vocabulary should be previewed at the beginning of the lesson and highlighted at the end of the lesson to reinforce learning,

-- advanced organizers,

-- use computers to help present material,

-- provide visual clues,

-- maintain good eye contact,

-- present more difficult lessons early in the day; children and teens with ADD fatigue more easily than others; also, their medication often wears off in the late morning (if they are taking the regular form of Ritalin or Dexedrine).

Materials

-- taped texts,

-- highlighted texts/study guides,

-- use supplementary materials as needed,

-- note taking assistance; carbon copies notes of regular student,

-- typed notes from the teacher,

-- use of calculators or computer word processors,

-- use adapted or simplified texts,

-- use graph paper for math problems, handwriting, etc.

Assignments

-- give directions in small, distinct steps,

-- allow copying from paper or book,

-- use written backup for oral instructions,

-- lower reading level of assignment,

-- adjust length of assignment,

-- change format of assignments to best fit need of child,

-- give assignments in chunks, or a series of smaller assignments,

-- reduce pencil and paper tasks,

-- read directions/worksheets to students,

-- give oral/visual clues or prompts,

-- allow assignments to be typed or dictated,

-- adapt worksheets/packets,

-- maintain an assignment notebook,

-- avoid penalizing for spelling errors,

-- encourage the use of dictation or computer word processing for those with writing difficulties.

** For people with visual processing problems, you may have them read their material into a tape recorder and then listen to the material over and over.

Reinforcement and Follow Through

-- reward systems for positive behavior,

-- use concrete rewards,

-- consistent, firm, unemotional consequences for unacceptable behavior,

-- check often for understanding and review,

-- peer tutoring,

-- request parental reinforcement if it is positive,

-- have student repeat the instructions,

-- make/use vocabulary files,

-- teach study skills,

-- teach organizational skills (and supervise their implementation on a regular basis),

-- use study sheets to organize material,

-- reinforce long-term assignment timeliness (cut into short chunks),

-- repeated review drills,

-- use behavioral contracts/daily or weekly report cards,

-- before and after school tutoring,

-- regular conferences with student and parents (emphasize the positive as well as giving feedback on the negative).

Testing Adaptations

-- oral,

-- taped,

-- read test to student,

-- reduce reading level,

-- adjust time for test completion,

-- short answer or multiple choice questions best,

-- shorten the length of test,

-- test for knowledge, not attention span.

Grading

-- modify weights of examination,

-- give extra credits for projects,

-- credit for appropriate class participation,

-- increase or eliminate time limits,

-- shorten length of exam.

Encourage Questions

-- take time to encourage the child or teen to ask questions when he or she feels confused or lost, confused or lost,

-- establish a positive feeling about asking questions. Most students do not ask questions for fear of appearing stupid. If they can overcome this barrier, it will serve them well for the rest of their academic career,

-- praise the child for asking appropriate questions.

Discipline

-- firm and kind are the words to remember,

-- when you say something, mean it and be willing to back it up, but in a kind, caring tone,

-- be very careful not to discipline a child when their misbehavior is the result of confusion or misunderstanding instructions,

-- use discipline for teaching, not punishment,

-- never discipline a child when you feel you're out of control,

-- show disapproval of the behavior, not the child,

-- stay calm and unemotional (remember, ADD children are often trying to get a rise out of you!),

-- have well-thought-out consequences to certain behaviors ahead of time (anticipation is the key to success),

-- focus 90% of your efforts with the child on noticing behavior you like, to set a positive tone,

-- have frequent contact with the parents (they need to be allied with you if discipline is going to be effective).

Finger Agnosia
(struggle with the mechanics of writing or
when you try to write your brain becomes scrambled)

This is very common in people with ADD and occurs in part because the person has to concentrate so hard on the actual physical act of writing that they forget or are unable to formulate what they want to write.

Common symptoms of finger agnosia include:

-- messy handwriting,

-- trouble getting thoughts from the brain to the paper,

-- staring at writing assignments for long periods of time,

-- writing sentences that don't make sense,

-- frequent spelling and grammatical errors,

-- many erasures and corrections,

-- timed writing assignments are particularly hard,

-- printing rather than writing in cursive,

Here are some helpful suggestions for dealing with finger agnosia:

-- print as often as possible (it's easier and uses less effort),

-- learn to type or use a computer word processor (Mavis' Teaches Typing is an excellent program for children and teens),

-- try out different types of pens and pencils to see which ones work best for you. Some are more help helpful than others,

-- break down assignments and long reports into parts, and work at them over time, rather than all at once (such as on the night before they are due),

-- before you do the actual writing project, write an outline of the assignment to help keep you on track.,

-- write down your ideas before worrying about spelling/grammar,

-- whenever possible, dictate your answer or report first. This often helps you add ideas and substance to the article that would not have been present through writing alone,

-- use a binder/organizer to keep your writing assignments together,

-- writing workloads at work and school need to be appropriately modified,

-- avoid timed situations; give tests orally if necessary,

-- avoid having other students grade the work (as this may set up embarrassment and teasing).

Taking the Nightmare out of Homework

-- provide a "special" quiet spot without distractions in which to do homework,

-- break into short segments of about 15 to 20 minutes, interspersed with physical activity, set a timer to structure work periods,

-- intersperse physical activity in breaks between segments,

-- check assignment sheets and notebooks teacher on a regular basis,

-- continually work on good communication between home and school,

-- reward positive homework behavior,

-- if problems continue, use a daily report system to ensure compliance.

Useless and/or Harmful Strategies

-- tell the child or teen to try harder (the harder they try, the worse it gets),

-- lecture a student about showing their "true" ability,

-- only notice the negative,

-- compare a student to other students.

DAILY PROGRESS NOTE (DPN)

Supervision is key to helping students with ADD or other students who are having difficulty transitioning to the rigors of school. They often have not developed the internal discipline to be successful day-to-day at school and with their homework. I use this system for both children and teenagers. Even though teenagers may balk at this system, many teens in my practice have used it very successfully. I'm convinced that many students have graduated from high school because we kept them on track with this system! ADD students tend to do much better if they know someone is watching.

Directions:

Every school day the child or teen is to bring the DAILY PROGRESS NOTE to school for the teacher or teachers to fill out (at the end of the day if there is only one teacher, at the end of each class for those who have multiple teachers). The teacher (or teachers) rates the student on a scale of 1 - 5 (1 = best, 5 = worst) in four different areas: homework, class participation, class work and peer interactions. After rating the child in each area, the teacher is then to put his or her initials at the bottom of the form. (It is important to emphasize to the teacher to give an accurate assessment. Some teachers give out "good" marks just to be nice and then put the real grades down on the report card, shocking the student and parents.)

At the end of the day, the child or teen brings the DPN home. This note provides the student, parents and teacher immediate feedback on performance and helps everyone track progress throughout the year. Good performance is noticed and reinforced. Mediocre or poor performance is observed and necessary corrective measures can be put into place. When the child or teen brings the DPN home, it is helpful if parents first look for something they like (too many parents only notice the negative). If the child or teen's marks are particularly poor, the parents need to question the reasons behind the difficulties of the day.

After the discussion, the parent then assigns points for the day.

Here is a sample point system:

1 = 5 points
2 = 2 points
3 = 1 point
4 & 5 = 0 points

In the system listed above (for students with one teacher a day), there is a total of 20 possible points that the child can earn (a score of 1 [5 points] multiplied by 4 areas = 20 points).

The points are then spent in two different ways. One, on daily wants and needs, the other for future privileges. Earning points for daily wants and needs is significant, as these reinforce and discipline behavior on a more immediate basis. To do this, the parent and child make up a list of the things he or she likes to do on a daily basis, such as watching television, playing outside, having a friend over, playing a video game, talking on the telephone, etc. Half of the possible points (10 in the example above) should be spent on daily privileges. This lets the child know that he or she can't just blow a day at school and expect everything to be okay at home.

For example,

Points Needed for Daily Wants

2 = 1/2 hour of television
2 = 1 hour of playing outside
3 = having a friend over for an hour
2 = playing a video game
3 = 1/2 hour of telephone privilege

The other half of their points can be saved for special treats and privileges as they earn enough points (such as a special toy, a trip to their favorite restaurant, having a friend spend the night or being able to stay up past their bedtime). It is important to make up a "wish" list of the things the child or teen is willing to work for. The child or teen needs to develop this list in order to more fully buy into this program.

In some cases, children will intentionally lose their DPN or forget to have their teacher sign it if their performance that day was poor. In the case where the child claims to have lost the DPN or they say that the teacher didn't fill it out, they lose all of their points for the day (or portion of points if multiple teachers are involved). The child or teen must take responsibility! On a day where the child earns little or no points for various privileges, the child is to be encouraged to do better the next day and he or she is simply allowed to read books or play in his or her room.

Almost all children find this system to be very rewarding after they have used it for several days. Some children refuse to participate initially, but if the parents persist, the child will almost always give in. One of the advantages of this system is that some children become "miserly" with their points and will often give up watching television and playing video games to save points for other things they are interested in. In addition, many begin to develop a more positive attitude toward school because of their ability to earn extra privileges for performing well in school.

Some parents have asked me if the DPN does not single out the child for teasing from peers. I have rarely found this to be the case. In fact, this helps the child to modify their behavior in school, which in turns helps their interactions with peers.

DAILY PROGRESS NOTE

Name: _____ Date: _____
 Please rate this child/teen in each of the areas listed below as to how he/she performed in school today, using ratings of 1 - 5. 1 = excellent, 2 = good, 3 = fair, 4 = poor, 5 = terrible or did not do the work.

| | Class Periods/Subjects | | | | | | |
	1	2	3	4	5	6	7
Homework	[ ]	[ ]	[ ]	[ ]	[ ]	[ ]	[ ]
Class Participation	[ ]	[ ]	[ ]	[ ]	[ ]	[ ]	[ ]
Class Work	[ ]	[ ]	[ ]	[ ]	[ ]	[ ]	[ ]
Peer Interactions	[ ]	[ ]	[ ]	[ ]	[ ]	[ ]	[ ]
Teacher's Initials	[ ]	[ ]	[ ]	[ ]	[ ]	[ ]	[ ]

DAILY PROGRESS NOTE

Name: _____ Date: _____

Please rate this child/teen in each of the areas listed below as to how he/she performed in school today, using ratings of 1 - 5. 1 = excellent, 2 = good, 3 = fair, 4 = poor, 5 = terrible or did not do the work.

	Class Periods/Subjects						
	1	2	3	4	5	6	7
Homework	[ ]	[ ]	[ ]	[ ]	[ ]	[ ]	[ ]
Class Participation	[ ]	[ ]	[ ]	[ ]	[ ]	[ ]	[ ]
Class Work	[ ]	[ ]	[ ]	[ ]	[ ]	[ ]	[ ]
Peer Interactions	[ ]	[ ]	[ ]	[ ]	[ ]	[ ]	[ ]
Teacher's Initials	[ ]	[ ]	[ ]	[ ]	[ ]	[ ]	[ ]

DAILY PROGRESS NOTE

Name: _____ Date: _____

Please rate this child/teen in each of the areas listed below as to how he/she performed in school today, using ratings of 1 - 5. 1 = excellent, 2 = good, 3 = fair, 4 = poor, 5 = terrible or did not do the work.

	Class Periods/Subjects						
	1	2	3	4	5	6	7
Homework	[ ]	[ ]	[ ]	[ ]	[ ]	[ ]	[ ]
Class Participation	[ ]	[ ]	[ ]	[ ]	[ ]	[ ]	[ ]
Class Work	[ ]	[ ]	[ ]	[ ]	[ ]	[ ]	[ ]
Peer Interactions	[ ]	[ ]	[ ]	[ ]	[ ]	[ ]	[ ]
Teacher's Initials	[ ]	[ ]	[ ]	[ ]	[ ]	[ ]	[ ]

Get School Resources Involved Early

Under the law (PL 94-142) all students are entitled to an educational setting where they can learn. If they are handicapped, the school system must make proper modifications so that they can receive an education. As you have seen, ADD often handicaps a child or teen from taking advantage of education. Do to a lack of funding and personnel, however, many schools overlook children with ADD and learning problems unless they are forced to take action. Parents need to be the prime force that gets the child appropriate help.

Parents need to ADVOCATE for their children and not just rely on the overworked principal, counselor or school psychologist. To that end, parents must be educated on ADD and know the proper school interventions. I often tell my parents that they are the ones who need to intervene when things are not going well at school. The squeaky wheel gets the grease! Don't give in to a school administrator who tries to intimidate you! Who is condescending to you.

If you are not the "assertive type," consider obtaining a school advocate for your child. A school advocate is someone who has experience in dealing with the school system to ensure the child gets all the help he or she needs. To get the name of an advocate in your area contact the local chapter of CH.A.D.D. (a national support group for parents of children with ADD with local chapters) or the Disability Rights Education and Defense Fund in Berkeley, California at (510) 644-2555.

Most school systems are willing to test preschool children if there is a suspected learning or speech problem. Contact your local school counselor or principal for more information on special testing. The earlier you address problems, the more hope there is for successful interventions. Also, see the section under "Understanding The Law And ADD" in Chapter 30 to further understand your rights.

CHAPTER 26

Brainwave Biofeedback

GOAL:

increase <u>beta</u> or concentration level of activity

decrease <u>theta</u> or daydreaming level of activity

Medication is the cornerstone of the "biological" treatments for ADD, but it is not the only treatment. Over the past 15 years, Joel Lubar, Ph.D., of the University of Tennessee and other researchers have reported the effectiveness of a new tool in the treatment of ADD. This treatment tool is brainwave or EEG biofeedback. Biofeedback, in general, is a treatment technique which utilizes instruments to measure physiological responses in a person's body (such as hand temperature, sweat gland activity, breathing rates, heart rates, blood pressure and brain wave patterns). The instruments then feed the information on these body systems to the patient who can then learn how to change them. In brainwave biofeedback, the level of specific brainwave patterns are measured throughout the brain.

There are five types of brainwave patterns:

** **delta brainwaves** (1-4 cycles per second), which are very slow brainwaves, seen mostly during sleep;

** **theta brainwaves** (5-7 cycles per second), which are slow brainwaves, seen during daydreaming and twilight states;

** **alpha brainwaves** (8-12 cycles per second), which are brainwaves seen during relaxed states;

** **SMR (sensorimotor rhythm)** brainwaves (12-15 cycles per second), which are brainwaves seen during states of focused relaxation

** **beta brainwaves** (13-24 cycles per second), which are fast brainwaves seen during concentration or mental work states.

In evaluating over 1200 children with ADHD, Dr. Lubar has found that the basic problem with these children is that they lack the ability to maintain "beta" concentration states for sustained periods of time. He also found that these children have excessive "theta" daydreaming brainwave activity. Dr. Lubar found that through the use of EEG biofeedback, children could be taught to increase the amount of "beta" brainwaves and decrease the amount of "theta" or daydreaming brainwaves.

The basic biofeedback technique has children, teens or adults play games with their minds. The more they can concentrate and produce "beta" states the more rewards they can accrue. On the EEG biofeedback equipment, for example, a child sits in front of a computer monitor and watches a game screen. If he increases the "beta" activity or decreases the "theta" activity, the game continues. The games stops, however, when they are unable to maintain those brainwave states. Children find the screens fun and many are able to gradually shape their brainwave patterns to a more normal one. From experience, clinicians know that this treatment technique is not an overnight cure. Children often have to do this form of biofeedback for between one to two years.

In my experience with EEG biofeedback and ADD, many people are able to improve their reading skills and decrease their need for medication. Also, EEG biofeedback has helped to decrease impulsivity and aggressiveness. It is a powerful tool, in part, because we are making the patients part of the treatment process by giving them more control over their own physiological processes.

The use of brainwave biofeedback is considered controversial by many clinicians and researchers. More published research needs to be done in order to demonstrate its effectiveness. Also, in some circles EEG biofeedback has been oversold. Some clinics have advertised the ability to cure ADD with biofeedback and without the use of medication. Unfortunately, overselling this treatment technique has hurt its credibility. Still, in my clinical experience, I find EEG biofeedback to be a powerful and exciting treatment and we are yet to see its full development.

Audio-Visual Stimulation

A similar treatment to EEG biofeedback is something called Audio-Visual Stimulation. This technique was developed by Harold Russell, Ph.D. and John Carter, Ph.D., two psychologists at the University of Texas, Galveston. Both Drs. Russell and Carter were involved in the treatment of ADD children with EEG biofeedback. They wanted to develop a treatment technique that could be available to more children.

Based on a concept termed "entrainment," where brainwaves tend to pick up the rhythm in the environment, they develop special glasses and headphones which flashes lights and sounds at a person at specific frequencies which help the brain "tune in" to be more focused. Patients wear these glasses for 30-45 minutes a day.

I have tried this treatment on a number of patients with some encouraging results. One patient, who developed tics on both Ritalin and Dexedrine, tried the glasses for a month. His ADD symptoms significantly improved. When he went off the Audio-Visual Stimulator, his symptoms returned. The symptoms again subsided when he retried the treatment.

I believe that both EEG biofeedback and Audio-Visual Stimulation techniques show promise for the future, but more research is needed.

CHAPTER 27

Goal-Directed
Psychotherapy Techniques

Without the proper medical treatment, psychotherapy can be a fruitless and frustrating experience for both the therapist and patient. I have consulted with many ADD patients who have been in psychotherapy for years without much benefit. When they were placed on the right medication, however, dramatic improvement occurred in several weeks. This is not to say that psychotherapy is not a necessary component of treatment for children, teen and adults with ADD. It is often very helpful, but it needs to be in combination with the right medical treatment, as ADD is a neurobiological disorder. Here are some of the following psychotherapy themes that are essential in dealing with the ADD patient.

Break Up Erroneous Belief Patterns

Many people with ADD may have erroneous, negative beliefs that prevent them from being successful in the present. For example, they may believe that they'll fail in school (because that was their experience before they were treated) so they will not try. Or, they may believe that they are doomed to have poor relationships (again, because that was their experience before treatment), so they will engage in the same, repetitive behaviors that impair their ability to relate to others. Once medical treatment is successful, it is also important to correct these beliefs, because beliefs drive behavior.

Willie was impotent as an adult. In treatment, I hypnotized him back to the first time he lost his erection with his wife prematurely. He remembered feeling inadequate and ashamed. Still in the hypnotic trance, I asked him to remember the first time in his whole life that he felt inadequate and ashamed. He started to cry and told me of a time when he was six years old. His father was yelling at him and called him "stupid" because he was unable to learn to read! He transferred the feelings of shame and inadequacy to his sexual life as an adult and still felt incompetent. In the hypnotic trance, I educated his unconscious mind about ADD and the erroneous beliefs he carried into adulthood. I told him to rethink his basic assumptions and have his mind help him rather than hurt him. The impotence disappeared within a month.

Along similar lines, Adrianne never played cards. As a child and teenager, she had trouble learning card games because her attention span was so short. When she did play, her impulsiveness caused her to make bad decisions and she often lost at cards, even though she was just as smart or smarter than her opponent. As an adult, she avoided social situations where card games were played. This caused turmoil in her marriage because her husband liked to play cards with other couples and she refused to go with him. After she was placed on medication, she still avoided playing cards until she began talking about this in therapy. When she made the connection between ADD and her underlying belief about card games, she was able to challenge herself to try again. She found out that she really liked playing cards, and she began to go with her husband.

Accept The Need For Medication

Medication often becomes a psychotherapy issue. Many people do not want to believe that there is anything wrong with them and taking the medication may make them feel, in some way, defective. It is critical to talk about these feelings. When these feelings are ignored, children, teens and adults start missing doses of medication and then it loses its overall effectiveness. Justine was an example of this. At age 22 her life was falling apart. She had taken Ritalin as a teenager and it was very helpful for her. However, in the 12th grade a friend teased her about the medication, and she stopped it. Within the next year, she had been arrested twice for shoplifting, started using drugs, and had dropped out of high school. The next four years were nothing but trouble. After she saw a special on television about adult ADD, she remembered how helpful the medication had been for her and she sought help. After she was placed back on the medication, she was able to start college, maintain stable work and avoid antisocial behavior.

Therapy For Thoughts

Children, teens and adults with ADD often develop erroneous thought patterns, based on the numerous failures they have experienced in their lives. It is often very helpful to investigate they way an ADD person thinks and then teach them to correct any erroneous thought patterns.

Here are some examples of common negative thoughts.

"I'm a terrible student."

"I'm always messing things up."

"No one ever wants to be with me."

"Anybody could have done that. I'm not so special."

"The teacher (or boss) doesn't like me."

"I will fail at this....."

"I feel you don't love me."

"I should do better."

"I'm so stupid."

These thoughts severely limit a person's ability to enjoy his or her life. How people think "moment by moment" has a huge impact on how they feel and how they behave. Negative thoughts often drive difficult behaviors and cause people to have problems with their self-esteem. Hopeful thoughts, on the other hand, influence positive behaviors and lead people to feel good about themselves and be more effective in their day-to-day lives.

Most ADD children, teens and adults have a lot of negative thoughts. These thoughts come from many sources. Some of the negative thoughts come from what other people have told them about themselves (i.e., "You're no good! Why can't you ever listen? What's the matter with you? You make me crazy!"). Other negative thoughts originate from experiences where the person is continually frustrated, either at home, school or work. They begin to think thoughts such as, "I'm stupid. I can't ever do anything right. It will never work out for me."

In many ways, our brain works like a computer. When a person receives negative INPUT about themselves, they STORE it in their subconscious mind and they then EXPRESS those messages in their negative behavior or feelings. Unless people are taught how to talk back to these harmful thoughts and messages, they believe them unconditionally. This is a critical point. Most people never challenge the thoughts that go through their heads. They never even think about their own thoughts. They just believe what they think, even though the thoughts may be very irrational. Their behavior is often based on false assumptions or false ideas.

Many children have trouble thinking logically, because of their age (although this seems to be a common adult problem as well). Unfortunately, many ADD children carry these negative thought patterns into adulthood, causing them to have problems with their moods and behavior. These negative thoughts affect their moods and in many children become the seeds of anxiety or depression later on in life. It's critical to teach people about their thoughts and to teach them to challenge what they think, rather than just accepting thoughts blindly. Unfortunately, when you're a child, no one teaches you to think much about your thoughts or to challenge the notions that go through your head, even though your thoughts are always with you. Why do we spend so much time teaching kids about diagraming sentences and so little time teaching them how to think clearly? Most people do not understand how important thoughts are, and leave the development of thought patterns to random chance. Did you know that thoughts have actual weight and mass? They are real! They have significant influence on every cell in your body (more detail on this in a little bit). When a person's mind is burdened with many negative thoughts, it affects their ability to learn, their ability to relate to other people and their physical health. Teaching people with ADD how to control and direct their thoughts in a positive way can be helpful in all areas of their lives.

Here are the actual step-by-step "positive thinking" principles that I use in my psychotherapy practice with children, teens and adults. When people truly learn these principles, they gain more control over their feelings and their behavior.

STEP #1: Did you know...Every time you have a thought your brain releases chemicals. That's how our brain works.

you have a thought,

your brain releases chemicals,

an electrical transmissions goes across your brain and

you become aware of what you're thinking.

Thoughts are real and they have a real impact on how you feel and how you behave.

STEP #2: Every time you have a mad thought, an unkind thought, a sad thought, or a cranky thought, your brain releases negative chemicals that make your body feel bad. Whenever you're upset, imagine that your brain releases bubbles with sad or angry faces, looking to cause problems. Think about the last time you were mad. What did you feel inside your body? When most people are mad, their muscles get tense, their heart beats faster, their hands start to sweat and they may even begin to feel a little dizzy. Your body reacts to every negative thought you have.

STEP #3: Every time you have a good thought, a happy thought, a hopeful thought or a kind thought your brain releases chemicals that make your body feel good. Whenever you're happy, imagine that your brain releases bubbles with glad or smiling faces, making you feel good. Think about the last time you had a really happy thought (such as when you got a good grade on a test or cuddled a child). What did you feel inside your body? When most people are happy their muscles relax, their heart beats slower, their hands become dry and they breathe slower. Your body also reacts to your good thoughts.

STEP #4: Your body reacts to every thought you have! We know this from polygraphs or lie detector tests. During a lie detector test, you are hooked up to equipment which measures:

hand temperature,
heart rate,
blood pressure,
breathing rate,
muscle tension and
how much the hands sweat.

The tester then asks questions, such as, "Did you do that thing?" If you did the bad thing your body is likely to have a "stress" response and it is likely to react in the following ways:

hands get colder,
heart goes faster,
blood pressure goes up,
breathing gets faster,
muscles get tight and
hands sweat more.

Almost immediately, the body reacts to what you think, whether you say anything or not. Now the opposite is also true. If you did not do what they are asking you about it is likely that your body will experience a "relaxation" response and react in the following ways:

hands will become warmer,
heart rate will slow,
blood pressure goes down,
breathing becomes slower and deeper,
muscles become more relaxed and
hands become drier.

Again, almost immediately, your body reacts to what you think. This not only happens when you're asked about telling the truth, your body reacts to every thought you have, whether it is about school, friends, family or anything else.

STEP #5: Thoughts are very powerful! They can make your mind and your body feel good or they can make you feel bad! Every cell in your body is affected by every thought you have. That is why when people get emotionally upset they actually develop physical symptoms, such as headaches or stomachaches. Some people even think that people who have a lot of negative thoughts are more likely to get cancer. If you can think about good things you will feel better. Did you know that Abraham Lincoln had periods of bad depression when he was a child and adult? He even thought about killing himself and had some days when he didn't even get out of bed. In his later life, however, he learned to treat his bad feelings with laughter. He became a very good story teller and loved to tell jokes. He learned that when he laughed, he felt better. Over a hundred years ago, some people knew that thoughts were very important.

STEP #6: Unless you think about your thoughts, they are "automatic" or "they just happen." Since they just happen, they are not always correct. Your thoughts do not always tell you the truth. Sometimes they even lie to you. I once knew a boy who thought he was stupid because he didn't do well on tests. When we tested his IQ (intelligence level), however, we discovered that he was close to a genius! You don't have to believe every thought that goes through your head. It's important to think about your thoughts to see if they help you or they hurt you. Unfortunately, if you never challenge your thoughts, you just "believe them" as if they were true.

STEP #7: You can train your thoughts to be positive and hopeful or you can just allow them to be negative and upset you. Once you learn about your thoughts, you can chose to think good thoughts and feel good, or you can choose to think bad thoughts and feel lousy. That's right, it's up to you! You can learn how to change your thoughts and you can learn to change the way you feel.

One way to learn how to change your thoughts is to notice them when they are negative and talk back to them. If you can correct negative thoughts, you take away their power over you. When you just think a negative thought without challenging it, your mind believes it and your body reacts to it.

STEP #8: As I mentioned above, negative thoughts are mostly automatic or they "just happen." I call these thoughts "Automatic Negative Thoughts. If you take the first letter from each of these words, it spells the word ANT. Think of these negative thoughts that invade your mind like ants that bother people at a picnic. One negative thought, like one ant at a picnic, is not a big problem. Two or three negative thoughts, like two or three ants at a picnic, becomes more irritating. Ten or twenty negative thoughts, like ten or twenty ants at a picnic, can cause real problems.

Whenever you notice these automatic negative thoughts or ANTs you need to crush them or they'll begin to ruin your whole day. One way to crush these ANTs is to write down the negative thought and talk back to it. For example, if you think, "Other kids will laugh at me when I give my speech" write it down and then write down a positive response; something like "The other kids will like my speech and find it interesting." When you write down negative thoughts and talk back to them, you take away their power and help yourself feel better. Some kids tell me they have trouble talking back to these negative thoughts because they feel that they are lying to themselves. Initially, they believe that the thoughts that go through their mind are the truth. Remember, thoughts sometimes lie to you. It's important to check them out before you just believe them!

Here are nine different ways that our thoughts lie to us to make situations out to be worse than they really are. Think of these nine ways as different species or types of ANTs (automatic negative thoughts). When you can identify the type of ANT, you begin to take away the power it has over you. I have labeled some of these ANTs as red, because these ANTs are particularly harmful to you. Notice and exterminate ANTs whenever possible.

ANT #1: All or nothing thinking: These thoughts happen when you make something out to be all good or all bad. There's nothing in between. You see everything in black or white terms. The thought for children, "There's nothing to do," is an example of this. When children say "There's nothing to do" they feel down and upset, bored and unmotivated to change the situation. But is, "There's nothing to do," a rational thought? Of course not, it's just a thought. Even on a day when it's raining outside and children have to stay in, they can probably list 20 things to do if they put your mind to it such as: draw, make paper airplanes, write a story, read a story, do a puzzle, write grandma a letter, play hide and seek, do chores, write a novel thought, etc. But if they never challenge the thought, "There's nothing to do," they just believe it and spend the rest of the day feeling crummy. Other examples of "all or nothing thinking" include thoughts such as, "I'm the worst ball player in the city. If I get an A on this test, I'm a great student, but if I do poorly, then I'm no good at all."

ANT #2: "Always" thinking: This happens when you think something that happened will "always" repeat itself. For example, if your wife is irritable and she gets upset you might think to yourself, "She's always yelling at me," even though she yells only once in a while. But just the thought "She's always yelling at me" is so negative that it makes you feel sad and upset. Whenever you think in words like always, never, no one, everyone, every time, everything those are examples of "always" thinking and usually wrong. There are many examples of "always" thinking: "No one ever plays with me. Everyone is always picking on me. You never listen to me. You always give her what she wants." This type of ANT is very common. Watch out for it.

ANT #3 (red ANT): Focusing on the negative: This occurs when your thoughts only see the bad in a situation and ignore any of the good that might happen. For example, if you have to move, even though you're sad to leave your friends, you don't think of the new places you'll see and the new friends you'll make. It's very important, if you want to keep your mind healthy, to focus on the good parts of your life a lot more than the bad parts. I once helped a child who was depressed. In the beginning, he could only think about the bad things that happened to him. He had recently moved to my city and told me that he would never have friends (even though he already had several), he thought he would do poorly in his new school (even though he got mostly good grades) and that he would never have any fun (even though he lived near a bay and an amusement park). By focusing on the negative in his new situation, he was making it very hard on himself to adjust to his new home. He would have been much better off if he looked at all the positives in the situation rather than the negatives.

Negative people can learn a powerful lesson from the Disney movie, "Pollyanna." In the movie, Pollyanna comes to live with her aunt after the death of her missionary parents. Even though she had lost her parents, she was able to help many "negative people" with her attitude. She introduced them to the "glad game," to look for things to be glad about in any situation. Her father had taught her this game after she experienced a disappointment. She had always wanted a doll, but her parents never had enough money to buy it for her. Her father sent a request for a secondhand doll to his missionary sponsors. By mistake, they sent her a pair of crutches. "What is there to be glad about crutches," she thought. Then she decided she could be glad because she didn't have to use them. This very simple game changed the attitudes and lives of many people in the movie. The minister was especially affected by Pollyanna. Before she came to town he preached hellfire and damnation, but he did not seem to be very happy. Pollyanna told him that her father said that the Bible had 800 "Glad Passages," and that if God mentioned being glad that many times, it must be because He wants us to think that way. Focusing on the negative in situations will make you feel bad. Playing the glad game, or looking for the positive, will help you feel better.

ANT #4 (red ANT): Fortune telling: This is where you predict the worst possible outcome to a situation. For example, before you have to give a speech in front of a class or work meeting, you might say to yourself, "Other people will laugh at me or think I'm stupid." Just having this thought will make you feel nervous and upset. I call "fortune telling" red ANTs because they really hurt your chances for feeling good.

I once treated a 10-year-old boy named Kevin who stuttered in class whenever he read out loud. In private, he was a wonderful reader, but whenever he started to read in class he thought to himself, "I'm a lousy reader; the other kids will laugh at me." Because he had these thoughts, he stopped raising his hand to volunteer to read. In fact, this thought made him so upset that he started getting sick before school, and missed nearly a month of school before his mother brought him to see me. He also stopped answering the telephone at home for fear that he would stutter whenever he said hello. When he told me about his thoughts in class and at home, I understood the problem. When you predict that bad things will happen, such as you will stutter, your mind then often makes them happen. For this child, when he saw himself stuttering in his mind, he then stuttered whenever he read in class. The treatment for Kevin was to get him to replace those negative thoughts and pictures in his head with the image of him being a wonderful reader in class. I also taught him to breathe slowly when he read and to think good thoughts. I also made him the designated person to answer the telephone at home. Whenever you're afraid of unreasonable things (such as answering the telephone or reading in class), it is important to face your fears. Otherwise, fears develop power over you. Over the next couple of weeks, he was able to go back to school, and he even volunteered to read. At home, his mother told me that he ran to answer the telephone whenever it rang. If you are going to predict anything at all, it is best to predict the best. It will help you feel good and it will help your mind make it happen.

ANT #5 (red ANT): Mind reading: This happens when you believe that you know what another person is thinking when they haven't even told you. Many people do mind reading, and more often than not it gets them into trouble. It is the major reason why people have trouble in relationships. I tell people,

"Please don't read anybody's mind; I have enough trouble reading it myself!" You know that you are doing mind reading when you have thoughts such as, "Those people are mad at me. They don't like me. They were talking about me."

I once treated a teenager, Dave, who had this problem so badly that he would hide in clothes racks at the shopping mall so that other kids wouldn't see him. He told me, "If they see me, they'll think I look funny and then they'll want to tease me." He became very nervous around other people, because he worried about what others thought of him. He finally realized that other teenagers were more worried about themselves and they really spent little time thinking about him. Avoid reading anyone's mind. You never know what they are thinking.

ANT #6: Thinking with your feelings: This occurs when you believe your negative feelings without ever questioning them. Feelings are very complex, and, as I mentioned above, feelings sometimes lie to you. But many people believe their feelings even though they have no evidence for them. "Thinking with your feelings" thoughts usually start with the words "I feel." For example, "I feel like you don't love me. I feel stupid. I feel like a failure. I feel nobody will ever trust me." Whenever you have a strong negative feeling, check it out. Look for the evidence behind the feeling. Do you have real reasons to feel that way? Or, are you feelings based on events or things from the past?

Here's an example. Matt, age 10, had a problem learning. He also got expelled from his school for fighting. He felt that he was stupid and that he was a bad boy. When I first met him, I diagnosed ADD and started him on medication. He also went to a new school. He did wonderful! He did so well, in fact, that his old school (which was a better school) was willing to take him back. When his mother told him this good news, he became very upset. He said that he felt that he would fail and have lots of problems. He was letting the "old" feelings from the past mess up his chances for a new start. When he corrected his negative feelings by talking back to them, he was able to return to his old school. He even made the honor roll!

ANT #7: Guilt beatings: Guilt is not a helpful emotion. In fact, guilt often causes you to do those things that you don't want to do. Guilt beatings happen when you think with words like "should, must, ought or have to." Here are some examples: "I should be nice to my younger brother. I must never lie. I ought to call my grandmother. I have to do my homework." Because of human nature, whenever we think that we "must" do something, no matter what it is, we don't want to do it. Remember the story of Adam and Eve. The only restriction that God put on them when he gave them the Garden of Eden was that they shouldn't eat from the Tree of Knowledge. Almost immediately after God told them what they "shouldn't do," they started to wonder why they shouldn't do it. Well, you know the rest of the story. They ate from the tree and ended up being tossed from the Garden of Eden. It is better to replace "guilt beatings" with phrases like "I want to do this...It fits my goals to do that...It would be helpful to do this.... So in our examples above, it would be helpful to change those phrases to "I want be nice to my younger brother. It's helpful for me not to lie, because people will trust me. I want to call my grandmother. It's in my best interest to do my homework."

ANT #8: Labeling: Whenever you attach a negative label to yourself or to someone else you stop your ability to take a clear look at the situation. Some examples of negative labels are "nerd, jerk, idiot, spoiled brat and clown." Negative labels are very harmful. Whenever you call yourself or someone else a spoiled brat or an idiot you lump that person in your mind with all of the "spoiled brats" or "idiots" that you've ever known and you become unable to deal with them in a reasonable way. Stay away from negative labels.

ANT #9 (the most poisonous red ANT): Blame: People who ruin their own lives have a strong tendency to blame other people when things go wrong in their life. They take little responsibility for their problems. When something goes wrong at home, school or work, they try to find someone to blame. They rarely admit their own problems. Typically, you'll hear statements from them like:

> "It wasn't my fault that...."
> "That wouldn't have happened if you had...."
> "How was I supposed to know...."
> "It's your fault that...."

The bottom line statement goes something like this: "If only you had done something differently then I wouldn't be in the predicament I'm in. It's your fault, and I'm not responsible."

Blaming others starts early. I have three children. When my youngest,

Katie, was 18 months old she would blame her brother, who was 11, for any trouble she might be in. Her nickname for him was DiDi, and "Didi did it," even if he wasn't home. One day she spilled a drink at the table while her mother's back was turned. When her mother turned around and saw the mess and asked what had happened, Katie told her that "Didi spilled my drink." When her mother told her that her brother was at a friend's house, Katie persisted that "Didi did it."

Whenever you blame someone else for the problems in your life, you become powerless to change anything. Many kids play the "Blame Game," but it rarely helps them. Stay away from blaming thoughts and take personal responsibility to change the problems you have.

Summary of ANT Types:

1. **All or nothing thinking**: thoughts that are all good or all bad.

2. **"Always" thinking**: thinking in words like always, never, no one, everyone, every time, everything.

3. **Focusing on the negative**: only seeing the bad in a situation.

4. **Fortune telling**: predicting the worst possible outcome to a situation with little or no evidence for it.

5. **Mind reading**: believing that you know what another person is thinking even though they haven't told you.

6. **Thinking with your feelings**: believing negative feelings without ever questioning them.

7. **Guilt beatings**: thinking in words like "should, must, ought or have to."

8. **Labeling**: attaching a negative label to yourself or to someone else.

9. **Blame**: blaming someone else for the problems you have.

Whenever you notice an ANT entering your mind, train yourself to recognize it and write it down. When you write down automatic negative thoughts (ANTs) and talk back to them, you begin to take away their power and gain control over your moods.

Here are some examples of ways to kill these ANTs:

ANT	Species of ANT	Kill the ANT
There's nothing to do.	All or Nothing	There are probably lots of things to do if I think about it for a little while.
No one ever plays with me.	Always Thinking	That's silly. I have played with lots of kids in my life.
The boss doesn't like me.	Mind Reading	I don't know that. Maybe she's just having a bad day. Bosses are people, too.
The whole class will laugh at me.	Fortune Telling	I don't know that. Maybe they'll really like my speech.
I'm stupid.	Labeling	Sometimes I do things that aren't too smart, but I'm not stupid.
It's my fault.	Blame	I need to look at my part of wife's the problem and look for ways I can make the situation better.

Your thoughts and the thoughts of your children matter. Teach them to be positive and it will benefit their mind and their bodies. Take time to teach yourself and your kids how to think positive and feel good.

Anger Control

Some researchers say that up to 85% of people with ADD have rage attacks. It is essential to teach these people how to have better control over their anger and temper. Anger can destroy relationships between couples, between parent and child, and it can affect friendships and work relationships. I give each of my patients who have a problem with anger an "Anger Management Plan." The plan contains the following five components:

One: Focus is essential. Before you do or say anything, ask yourself if your intended behavior fits with the goals you have for your life. For example, if you get angry at your wife and think of telling her off, ask yourself if that behavior is going to help you have a kind, caring, loving, supportive relationship with her (which is probably your goal). Thinking before you act is critical to managing anger.

Two: Correct negative thoughts. As mentioned above, negative thought patterns can cause anger, depression and disappointment. Whenever you feel anger well up inside of you, write down the thoughts that drive your feelings. Odds are, they are a little irrational. Correcting them will give you more control of the situation.

Three: Get away from the situation until you calm down. Distraction is often very helpful in defusing angry situations. I have many of my patients who have trouble with anger write out "TEN THINGS TO DO WHEN I GET MAD." Here is a sample list from a ten-year-old. Adapt it for your own needs.

1. Listen to music.
2. Hit my punching bag.
3. Play a video game.
4. Go to my bedroom and do my breathing.
5. Play with my toys, such as the army men.
6. Go out in the back yard and play.
7. Water my plants.
8. Watch TV.
9. Go to the garage and work with my tools.

10. Write about what I'm thinking and show it to Dr. Amen.

Four: Breathe slowly and deeply, mostly with your belly. The purpose of breathing is to get oxygen from the air into your body and to blow off waste products such as carbon dioxide. Every cell in your body needs oxygen in order to function. Brain cells are particularly sensitive to oxygen, as they start to die within four minutes when they are deprived of oxygen. Slight changes in oxygen content in the brain can alter the way a person feels and behaves. When a person gets angry, his or her breathing pattern changes almost immediately. Their breathing becomes more shallow and the rate increases significantly (see diagram below). This breathing pattern is inefficient and the oxygen content in the angry person's blood is lowered. Subsequently, there is less oxygen available to a person's brain and they may become more irritable, impulsive and confused, causing them to make bad decisions (such as to yell, threaten or hit another person).

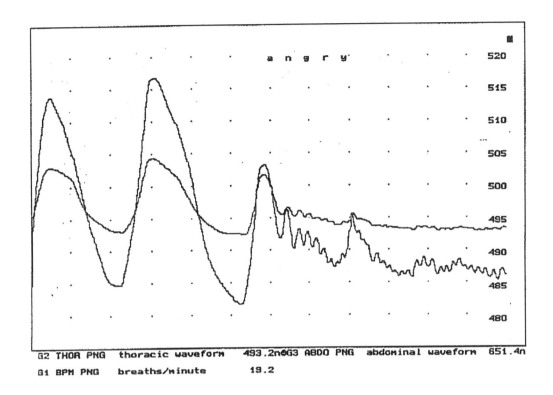

Breathing Diagram: The large waveform is a measurement of abdominal or belly breathing, by a gauge attached around the belly; the smaller waveform is a measurement of chest breathing, by a gauge attached around the upper chest. At rest, this person breathes mostly with his belly (a good pattern), but when he thinks about an angry situation his breathing pattern deteriorates, markedly decreasing the oxygen to his brain (common to anger outbursts). No wonder people who have anger outbursts often seem irrational!

To correct this negative breathing pattern, I teach my patients to become experts at breathing slowly and deeply, mostly with their bellies. In my office I have some very sophisticated biofeedback equipment that uses strain gauges to measure breathing activity. I place one gauge around a person's chest and a second one around their belly. The biofeedback equipment then measures the movement of the chest and belly as the person breathes in and out. Many people (especially men) breathe exclusively with their chest, which is an inefficient way to breathe. If you watch a baby or a puppy breathe, you notice that they breathe almost solely with their bellies. That is the most efficient way to breathe. If you expand your belly when you breathe in, it allows room for your lungs to inflate downward, increasing the amount of air available to your body. I then teach them to breathe with their bellies by watching their pattern on the computer screen. Over 20 - 30 minutes, most people can learn how to change their breathing patterns , which relaxes them and gives them better control over how they feel and behave.

If you do not have access to sophisticated biofeedback equipment, lie on your back and place a small book on your belly. When you breathe in, make the book go up, and when you breathe out, make the book go down. Shifting the energy of breathing lower in your body will help you feel more relaxed and in better control of yourself.

Five: Check medication schedules. Often, when a person with ADD loses control, it is at a time when the level of medication is low or non-existent in their body. It is essential to check dosage and timing of medication to see if there is a relationship between anger outbursts and medication.

CHAPTER 28

Specific Treatment Tips For Adults

Here are more tips that adults with ADD may find helpful.

Education:

** Learn as much about ADD as possible; don't rely on others; become informed.

** Educate others about ADD (spouse, children, family, friends). In that way they can become your ally, rather than being constantly frustrated by your behavior.

Note: before you notify an employer, evaluate his or her temperament and potential response to the information. Some employers will be very helpful and supportive; other employers might use the information against you.

** Join a support group if possible. This will put you in touch with the experience of others and also expose you to more information and coping styles. In a support group, you an also help others and by doing so help yourself. There are several support groups.

Psychological:

** Be sure to get treatment for any other underlying disorders, such as substance abuse, depression or anxiety.

** Reflect on the feedback others give you. If it is valid, use it to make yourself stronger.

** Notice your successes more than your failures.

** Learn from your failures, rather than letting them depress you.

Relational:

** Learn to actively listen to your partner. This involves clarifying what the other person says BEFORE you respond to them! Being an active listener will give you more stimulation and help you stay with the conversation.

** Schedule fun, especially if you have trouble fitting it into your day. Being balanced is essential to your feelings of success.

** Get the family involved in treatment if there are signs of family stress.

** Think before you speak!

Physical/Medical:

** Realize that ADD is biological and needs to be evaluated and treated like other biological illnesses, such as hypertension or diabetes.

** Exercise daily if possible, vigorously at least three times a week.

** Watch what you eat. Some adults react to certain food in a negative way, especially foods with additives or dyes.

** Go to bed at a reasonable time. If you have trouble sleeping, try a 6 ounce glass of warm milk with a tablespoon of vanilla and a tablespoon of sugar or honey to help you sleep.

** Many ADD people need two or three alarms to get them up in the morning. Set your clock radio to a station with fast-paced music. This will help turn your brain on. I have several patients who have actually gone to a security alarm company to get devices to wake them up in the morning.

** Watch the temptation to go off your medication because you're tired of taking it or because you just forget. Set up reminders in the environment (alarm watches, reminders from others, etc.) to help. Many ADD adults go off their meds and drive their spouses or employers NUTS.

** If you often forget your medication, ask your doctor for a slow release form

(Dexedrine's slow release form seems to be more reliable than Ritalin's, but I have good results with both).

Practical/Organizational:

** Make clear goals for your life in the following areas:

-- relationships (spouse/lover, children, family and friends)
-- work
-- money
-- physical health
-- emotional health
-- spirituality

Then ask yourself, "Is my behavior getting me what I want?" This critical exercise will help you stay on track in your life!

** Manage your time in a way that is consistent with the goals you have for your life.

** Take the extra time to organize your work area on a regularly scheduled basis. Devote some time each week to organization. Otherwise procrastination will take over.

** Use the FRAT system in organizing paper flow:

File it
Route it
Action
Throw it away

** Prioritize your projects.

** Make deadlines for yourself.

** Keep TO DO lists and revise them on a regular basis.
** Keep an appointment and planning book with you.

** Use a portable cassette recorder to remember ideas throughout the day.

** Break down large tasks into a series of smaller ones. Do a little each day on a certain project.

** Use file folders, desk organizers and labeled storage boxes to organize your paperwork.

Procrastination: Eight Ways To Beat It

1. Consciously fight procrastination. The sooner you do it, the sooner it will be done. If you can do it now, then do it now.

2. Break down overwhelming tasks into small tasks. This happens on assembly lines every day. Remember, "A journey of a thousand miles begins with one step."

3. Do a start-up task now! Go to the next step you need to do to accomplish that goal and do it. Just getting started will increase your momentum.

4. Make a wager with someone. Use your competitive nature to your advantage.

5. Give yourself a reward. Tell yourself that after you finish a difficult task, you'll reward yourself with something special you want.

6. Do unpleasant tasks first. That way, you'll have the more pleasurable ones to look forward to. If you save the unpleasant tasks for last, you'll have little incentive to get to them.

7. Tell someone else the date that you'll finish by. Putting your word or reputation on the line is often an incentive to get started.

8. Think about how you'd feel once the task is done. Anticipating the sense of accomplishment will help spur you on.

CHAPTER 29

Medication For ADD

Medication is most often an essential component to effective treatment for the ADD child, teen and adult. As I've said many times now, ADD is a neurobiological disorder and needs to be treated as such. Without the right medication, the other interventions are often very ineffective. During my child psychiatry training, my supervisors taught me to do play therapy with these children. It didn't work and I didn't care for these children. Who likes playing war, hour after hour, and listening to parents complain that the child is not any better? When these children are placed on the right medication, however, they can make very good use of their time in psychotherapy.

The goals of medication are to:

-- increase attention span and learning

-- decrease distractibility

-- decrease restlessness or high activity levels

-- decrease impulsiveness and increase thoughtfulness

-- decrease irritability

-- increase motivation

-- overall, improve functioning at school, at home, in relationships

and with the self.

In my experience, there are generally five classes of medication found to be effective in ADD, depending on the subtype I discussed above.

1. Stimulants:

methylphenidate (Ritalin)
dextroamphetamine (Dexedrine)
mixture of dextroamphetamine salts (Adderal)
methamphetamine (Desoxyn)
magnesium pemoline (Cylert)

** Contrary to popular belief, these are very safe medications
** with Cylert it is very important to monitor liver function tests, as 2-3% of people taking this medication may develop a chemical hepatitis

2. Tricyclic Antidepressants: (TCAs)

desipramine (Norpramin)
imipramine (Tofranil)
amitriptyline (Elavil)
nortryptiline (Pamelor)
clomipramine (Anafranil)

** these need to be monitored more closely than stimulants, especially their effect on heart function

* many adults respond to very low doses of these medications for ADD symptoms. This is important because the low doses often produce much fewer side effects than the higher "antidepressant" doses.

3. Antiobsessive or "anti-stuck" medications

fluoxetine (Prozac)
clomipramine (Anafranil)
(both a TCA and an anti-stuck medicine)
sertraline (Zoloft)
paroxetine (Paxil)
venlafaxine (Effexor)
fluvoxamine (Luvox)

** Contrary to the negative media attention, Prozac is generally a very safe medication with few side effects. In a very small percentage of patients it may cause them to become more irritable or more depressed, but that is true with all antidepressants. If there are side effects on any medication, it is important to contact your doctor and discuss them.

4. Anticonvulsants or anti-seizure medications:

> carbamazepine (Tegretol)
> valproic acid (Depakene or Depakote)

** it is important with these medications to watch the white blood cell counts and liver functions

** these are often helpful for people with ADD and violent outbursts or those who have experienced a head trauma

5. Blood pressure medications:

> clonidine (Catapres)
> guanfacine (Tenex)
> propranolol (Inderal)

** These mediations are often helpful to settle aggressiveness and/or hyperactivity.

Sometimes, a combination of medications is needed to obtain the full therapeutic effect. I particularly like the combination of stimulants and anti-obsessive medications for children of alcoholics.

The goal needs to be the best functioning, not to be off medication!!

Many people have the misguided belief that they will only take a "little bit" of the medication. Often this attitude causes the medication to be ineffective. I give patients the following metaphor:

When a person goes to the eye doctor because he or she is having trouble seeing, they want a prescription for the glasses that will help them see the best. They don't ask for "just a little bit of a lens," they want to see clearly!

So it is with ADD, everyone is different in the quantity of medication they require to function at their best. For some people, it is 5 milligrams of Ritalin two or three times a day. For others, it is 20 milligrams of Ritalin three or four times a day. Everyone is different.

The side effects of having ADD that is left untreated are immeasurably worse that those caused by the medication!

Common Questions
On The Use Of Stimulant Medication
for Attention Deficit Disorder

Stimulant medications include:

Ritalin (methylphenidate),
Dexedrine (dextroamphetamine),
Adderal (a mixture of dextroamphetamine salts),
Desoxyn (methamphetamine) and
Cylert (pemoline).

1. What Are The Indications For Stimulant Medications?

Stimulant medications have several uses in medicine. Most commonly, they are prescribed for ADD (both with and without hyperactivity). They are also used for narcolepsy (sudden sleep attacks), as an adjunctive treatment for depression, in chronic obesity, and to help thinking problems in the elderly.

2. How Can Stimulant Medications Help?

They can improve attention span, decrease distractibility, increase ability to finish tasks, improve ability to follow directions, decrease hyperactivity and restlessness, and lessen impulsivity. Handwriting often improves with this medication. School work, homework and overall work performance often improve significantly. Aggression and stubbornness is often lessened. Improved listening and communication skills often occur, along with a decrease in stimulation or conflict-seeking behaviors.

3. How Long Does The Medication Last? What Is The Usual Dosage?

Ritalin and Dexedrine usually last 3 to 4 hours, but in some people they last as little as 2 1/2 hours or as long as 6 hours. There is a slow-release form of Ritalin that lasts 6-8 hours and may help you or your child avoid taking a late morning or noontime dose. The slow-release form of Ritalin has a reputation for being somewhat erratic. For some people, it works great, for others, not so good. Often you just have to try it to see. The slow-release form of Dexedrine seems to be somewhat more reliable.

I usually prescribe medication for my patients in the afternoon and on weekends. During those times, people with ADD still need to do work, homework or housework and interact with other people.

Everyone is different in their need for medication. Some people need small doses (2 1/2 to 5 milligrams) of stimulant medication twice a day, some need it four or five times a day (this is where antidepressants have some advantage over the stimulants; most of them are only given once a day). Others needs larger doses of stimulants (15 to 20 milligrams); response often does not necessarily correlate with body weight. Trial, supervision and observation are the keys to finding the right dose.

4. How Will The Doctor Monitor The Medication?

In my practice, I initially see patients every couple of weeks until we find the right medication and dosage. During appointments, I ask about progress (at home, school and work) and check for any side effects of the medication. I'll keep a check on weight and height and occasionally check blood pressure. When Cylert is used, it is critical to check blood work for liver function before starting Cylert, and every couple of months thereafter. In addition, I often ask teachers to fill out follow-up rating scales to see the effectiveness of the medication. For adults, I often ask that their spouses come to the appointments so that I can get another opinion on the patient's progress.

5. What Side Effects Can These Medications Have?

Of all the medications I prescribe, stimulants, in my opinion, are the safest. I have never had to hospitalize a patient for a bad side effect and I have never had a side effect that did not go away once we stopped the medication.

Any medication can have side effects, including allergies to the medication (usually exhibited by a rash). Because each patient is different, it is important to work together with your physician to find the best medication with the least amount of side effects. The following list may not include rare or unusual side effects. Talk to your doctor if you or your child experiences anything different after starting the medication.

Common Side Effects

These often go away after about 2-3 weeks, or if the dose of the medication is lowered. Rarely, as the medication wears off there may be a rebound effect where the hyperactivity or moodiness becomes worse than before the medication was started. Dosage adjustments usually help rebound.

lack of appetite: Encourage a good breakfast, and afternoon and evening snacks, give medication after meals, rather than before. Some children and teen become hungry near bedtime. Unfortunately, some parents think that the child's hunger is no more than a manipulative ploy to stay up later, and engage the child or teen in a battle. The medication really does affect appetite. If the child or teen is hungry later on and they did not have much to eat at dinner, it is often a good idea to give them a late evening meal or snack. For some people, a lack of appetite is a significant problem and the medication may need to be changed or adjusted. Some of my patients use nutritional supplements, such as Ensure, to "ensure" they get enough calories and nutrients.

trouble falling asleep: Some people experience insomnia. If they do, I either give them a lower dose in the late afternoon or eliminate the last dose. In cases where there are problems when the last dose is eliminated, I may try giving a small dose of the stimulant right before bedtime. For insomnia, I often recommend a concoction of 6 ounces of warm milk with a tablespoon of vanilla and a tablespoon of sugar or honey. This seems to have a nice sedating effect for many people.

headaches or stomachaches: Commonly, patients may complain of headaches or stomachaches. These typically go away after several weeks. Tylenol and ibuprofen (Advil) seem to be helpful for the headaches; taking the medication with food often decreases the stomach problems.

irritability, crankiness, crying, emotional sensitivity, staring into space, loss of interest in friends: Some patients experience moodiness and minor personality changes. These side effects often go away in a week or two. If they don't, the medication often needs to be changed, maybe to an antidepressant.

Less Common Side Effects

tics: Some patients develop tics (such as eye blinking, throat clearing, head jerking) on the medication. If that happens, it is important to discuss it with your doctor. Sometimes the tics go away on their own; sometimes higher doses of the medication may improve the tics, and sometimes the medication has to be stopped. If the stimulant is very helpful, I might add another medication (such as clonidine or haloperidol) along with the stimulant to help with the tics. A complicating factor with tics, is that a high percentage of patients with tic disorders such as Gilles de la Tourette's Syndrome (manifested by having both motor and vocal tics) have ADD. Sometimes it is hard to know if the medication caused the tics or if the tics were already present, but worsened by the medication.

growth slowing: There use to be a concern about stimulants stunting growth, but the long term studies show that even though they may slow growth for a period of about a year, in the long run children usually catch up to where they should be.

rapid pulse or increased blood pressure: If a patient notices chest pain or a heart flutter it is important to notify the physician.

nervous habits: Picking at the skin, stuttering, and hair pulling can sometimes occur with these medications.

The side effects of having untreated ADD are immeasurably worse that those caused by the medication!

6. What Could Happen If This Medication Is Stopped Suddenly?

There are no medical problems to stopping the medication suddenly. A few people may experience irritability, moodiness, trouble sleeping or increased hyperactivity for a few days if they have been on daily medication for a long time. Often, it is better to stop the medication gradually over time (a week or so).

7. How Long Will The Medication Be Needed?

There is no way to know how long a person may need to take the medication. The patient, doctor, parent, teacher and spouse need to work together to find out what is right for each person. Sometimes the medication is only needed for a few years, sometimes it is needed for many years. Medication is an essential treatment for ADD, and until they outgrow it or find an alternative therapy that works (such as brainwave biofeedback), they need to remain on the medication. Without proper treatment, ADD is a serious disorder!

8. Does This Medication Interact With Other Medications?

It is a good idea to check with your doctor before mixing any prescription medications.

When they are used with tricyclic antidepressants they may cause confusion, irritability, hallucinations or emotional outbursts. Sometimes, however, combining stimulants with antidepressants can be a powerfully positive combination. I have done this in many patients without bad effects (everyone is different).

It is not a good idea to combine stimulants with nasal decongestants (such as medications that contain pseudoephedrine or related medications), because rapid pulse or high blood pressure may develop. If nasal decongestion is severe, it is better to use a nasal spray.

Many patients with ADD, may become cranky or more hyperactive on antihistamines (such as Benadryl). If medicine for allergies is needed, ask for one of the antihistamines that does not enter the brain (such as Hismanal).

Check with the pharmacist before giving any over-the-counter medication.

9. Does This Medication Stop Working At Puberty?

No! For most people it continues to work into adulthood. If it does lose its effectiveness, the dose may need to be increased or switching to another stimulant may be helpful. For the vast majority of people with ADD, it does not stop working at puberty (which many physicians used to tell parents).

10. Why Does This Medication Require A Special Prescription?

Prescriptions for Ritalin, Dexedrine and Desoxyn are written on special prescriptions known as "triplicates" (Cylert is written on a regular prescription). They must be filled within 7 days of the time the prescription is dated. Ritalin, Dexedrine and Desoxyn are controlled medications, because some adults have been known to abuse them. This is rare and I have never known any of my patients with ADD to have this problem while they were in treatment with me. In fact, the research shows that children who are adequately treated for ADD have a much lower percentage of drug abuse as teenagers and adults than those kids with ADD who were never treated with medication. This medication does not cause illegal drug use or addiction!

11. What If My Child Or I Have Problems Remembering To Take The Medication?

Remembering to take medication 3 - 5 times a day can be difficult, even for people who do not have ADD. Forgetfulness is a common symptom of ADD and when the medication has worn off, the person is fully ADD again. If forgetfulness is a chronic problem, don't blame or be upset. Look for solutions. Here are two solutions I recommend: try switching to a slow release form of the medication; or get an alarm system (such as an electronic watch with 5 alarms) to help you remember.

12. What About The Negative News Media Reports On These Medications?

It is critical to get your medical information from your doctor. Not Oprah, Geraldo or Phil. Many people have erroneous ideas about stimulant medication. If you hear things that worry you, check with your doctor before making any decisions.

Instructions On Starting Ritalin

Here are the instructions that I give to parents and adults starting stimulant medication. The following dosing pattern is for Ritalin. It differs for the other stimulants.

Over the next three weeks, please give Ritalin as follows:

week 1: one 5 mg. tablet three times a day (with breakfast, at lunch, and around 3:00 PM or 4:00 PM in the afternoon)

week 2: two 5 mg. tablet three times a day (with breakfast, at lunch, and around 3:00 PM or 4:00 PM in the afternoon)

-- if there is a problem with insomnia, you may want to give only one tablet in the afternoon.

week 3: three 5 mg. tablet three times a day (with breakfast, at lunch, and around 3:00 PM or 4:00 PM in the after noon)

-- if there is a problem with insomnia you may want to give only one or two tablets in the afternoon

** Each day, rate the child, teen or adult in mood and concentration on a scale of 1 - 10 (1 is terrible, 10 is great).

For children and teens it is often helpful to fill out a Conner's Parent-Teacher Rating Scale or similar rating scale to follow progress. This is to help us determine the best dosage of the medication.

** For children and teens, the school office will probably need a note from me allowing them to give the medication at school. Please make sure you get that from me. (sample note attached)

** If for some reason Ritalin does not seem to be effective, there are alternative medications for ADD. Always have hope!!

** When you have questions, please write them down so that we can talk about them at your next appointment. If you are ever worried or concerned about a side effect please do not hesitate to call me. I'd rather know sooner than later!

Sample Note To School Officials:

Stimulant Medication for Attention Deficit Disorder

Ritalin (methylphenidate)

Over the next three weeks please give Ritalin as follows:

week 1: one 5 mg. tablet at lunch

week 2: two 5 mg. tablet at lunch

week 3: three 5 mg. tablet at lunch

** After each week, please have the teacher fill out a Conner's Parent-Teacher Questionnaire, from the parents. This is to help us determine the best dosage of the medication.

** After the end of week three, please follow the instruction I give parents.

Thank You!

Daniel Amen, MD
Board Certified Physician in
Child, Adolescent and Adult Psychiatry

Checklist for Monitoring Medications

Date: _____ Name: _____ Age: _____ Sex: M/F_____

Checklist filled out by _____

Instructions: This checklist should be reviewed on a regular basis with your physician.

1. Medication(s), Dosages and Times:_____   _____

_____   _____

2. Attitudes about medication: (all that apply)

Adult's attitude about medication_____

Child's attitude about medication_____

Parents' attitude about medication _____

Teacher's attitude about medication _____

3. Progress Report On Target Symptoms: (all that apply)

	Improved	No Change	Worse
Hyperactivity/Restlessness	[]	[]	[]
Attention Span	[]	[]	[]
Distractibility	[]	[]	[]
Finishing Tasks	[]	[]	[]
Anger Control	[]	[]	[]
Frustration Tolerance	[]	[]	[]
Social Interactions			
home	[]	[]	[]
school	[]	[]	[]
friends	[]	[]	[]
Work Performance	[]	[]	[]
Compliance	[]	[]	[]
Handwriting	[]	[]	[]
Motivation	[]	[]	[]
Attitude	[]	[]	[]
Mood	[]	[]	[]
Anxiety Level	[]	[]	[]
Sleep	[]	[]	[]

Other (specify) _____

Other: _____

4. Have you noticed any of the following side effects?

[] loss of appetite

[] headaches/stomachaches

[] rashes

[] chest pain

[] fearfulness

[] tiredness or lethargy

[] constipation

[] other (specify) _____

[] tics or nervous habits

[] insomnia/other sleep changes

[] irritability/anger (time of day)____

[] moodiness or crying spells

[] social withdrawal

[] nervousness

[] blurred vision

[] weight changes

[] restlessness

[] dizziness

[] dark circles under the eyes

[] heart racing/skipping beats

[] dry mouth

[] sexual dysfunction

5. Please describe the time and frequency of the side effects:

_____

_____

6. Does the medication seem to help as much as you thought it would?

_____

_____

7. Have there been any problems remembering to take the medication

(where/what time of day)? _____

_____

8. Have you checked with others to see if they notice a difference? (teachers, spouse, friends, co-workers, etc.)

_____

_____

9. Physical Findings:

Height _____

Weight _____

* Pulse _____

* Blood Pressure _____

(* doctor will measure if he or she feels it's necessary)

10. Questions for the Doctor? _____

_____

MONTHLY MEDICATION RATING SHEET
Month_____

Name: _____   **Age:** _____

Medication(s)/dosage: _____

_____

_____

Please rate yourself or your child in the areas of concentration (C) and mood (M) on a scale of 1 - 10 (1 = terrible, 10 = great)

Dosage	Date/Day	Rating(C/M)	Dosage	Date/Day	Rating(C/M)
_____	_____	_____	_____	_____	_____
_____	_____	_____	_____	_____	_____
_____	_____	_____	_____	_____	_____
_____	_____	_____	_____	_____	_____
_____	_____	_____	_____	_____	_____
_____	_____	_____	_____	_____	_____
_____	_____	_____	_____	_____	_____
_____	_____	_____	_____	_____	_____
_____	_____	_____	_____	_____	_____
_____	_____	_____	_____	_____	_____
_____	_____	_____	_____	_____	_____
_____	_____	_____	_____	_____	_____
_____	_____	_____	_____	_____	_____
_____	_____	_____	_____	_____	_____
_____	_____	_____	_____	_____	_____
_____	_____	_____	_____	_____	_____
_____	_____	_____	_____	_____	_____
_____	_____	_____	_____	_____	_____
_____	_____	_____	_____	_____	_____
_____	_____	_____	_____	_____	_____
_____	_____	_____	_____	_____	_____

CHAPTER 30

The Law And ADD

There are basic protections provided to people with disabilities in the United States. The following is a summary of several pertinent laws and statutes. Do not take this as legal advice, but as a guideline to seek appropriate counsel when necessary.

The 5th and 14th Amendments of the Constitution

The 5th and 14th amendments of the Constitution provide for due process and equal protection of all citizens under the law. This includes protection for people with disabilities.

Individuals with Disabilities Act (IDEA)

The Individuals With Disabilities Act mandates that public school districts which receive federal funds must provide a "free appropriate public education" to children with disabilities.

Public Law 94-142

Public Law 94-142, which is also known as the Education for all Handicapped Children Act of 1975, is the federal law that states that every handicapped child has the right to a free and appropriate public education in the least restrictive environment. This law also provides that:

-- each handicapped child is guaranteed a culturally unbiased, valid assessment of his or her needs,

-- is to have an individualized education program designed to meet his or her unique needs,

-- is guaranteed specific procedures to insure his or her rights and those of parents (due process procedures).

The law says that all handicapped individuals need and have the right to an education in order to become self-sufficient and as productive as possible in adult society. Also, the handicapped children should be educated as much as possible with regular students (in the least restrictive environment).

The Rehabilitation Act of 1973 (RA)

The Rehabilitation Act of 1973 essentially outlaws discrimination against individuals with disabilities in education, employment (including federal government employment), and access to the benefits of federal programs by federal agencies and federal grant and contract recipients. Section 504 of this act defines the term disability.

The American With Disabilities Act (ADA)

The American With Disabilities Act outlaws discrimination against individuals with disabilities in private sector employment and state and local government activities and programs. It extends protection of the Rehabilitation Act of 1973 to individuals with disabilities who are employed by the Congress. Unlike the Rehabilitation Act of 1973, the ADA's protections do not depend on the receipt of federal funds.

In order to obtain the protections of the RA and ADA, it is necessary to establish that you: 1) are an "individual with a disability"; and 2) are "otherwise qualified"; and 3) were denied a job, education, or other benefit "solely by reason" of the disability; and 4) the individual, firm, or governmental agency which refused you is covered by the RA or ADA.

Under both the RA and ADA, an "individual with a disability" is any individual who:

(i) has a physical or mental impairment which substantially limits one or more of such person's major life activities,

(ii) has a record of such an impairment, or

(iii) is regarded as having such an impairment.

The second and third definitions are intended to protect individuals who previously had a disability but do not now, and those people who are treated as though they had a disability but do not.

The definition of a "physical or mental impairment" includes: "any mental or psychological disorder, such as mental retardation, organic brain syndrome, emotional or mental illness, and specific learning disabilities." Even though ADD is not specifically mentioned in the regulations, it is recognized as a "mental or psychological disorder." The effects of medication are not to be considered in assessing whether an individual has an "impairment." The severity of one's ADD or LD must meet these statutes without considering the potential benefits of medications.

The RA and ADA clearly apply to individuals with ADD and LD as long as these disorders substantially limit a major life activity, such as learning or job performance.

U. S. Education Department

On September 16, 1991 the U.S. Education Department issued a memorandum recognizing children with ADD as eligible for special education and related services under federal law. The policy makes clear that children with ADD qualify for special education and related services solely on the basis of ADD, when the ADD itself impairs educational performance or learning, under both (i) Public Law 94-142, Individuals with Disabilities Act (IDEA) statutes and regulations; and (ii) Section 504 of the 1973 Rehabilitation Act plus its implementing regulations. Schools are required to evaluate students suspected of having ADD and afford their families due process hearings in case there are disagreements over such evaluations. In addition, schools are required to have special education programs and services specifically designed for ADD education needs. It also requires regular classroom adaptations for children who do not need special education assistance.

Job Accommodations For ADD

Reasonable accommodations are required for workers who qualify under these statutes. Accommodations are of three general types:

1) those required to ensure equal opportunity in the job application process,

2) those which enable the individual with a disability to perform the essential features of a job, and

3) those which enable individuals with disabilities to enjoy the same benefits and privileges as those available to individuals without disabilities.

Reasonable accommodations for ADD and LD often include the following:

● providing or modifying equipment or devices
● job restructuring
● part-time or modified work schedules
● reassignment to a vacant position
● adjusting/modifying examinations, training materials, or policies
● providing readers or interpreters, and
● making the workplace accessible to and usable by people with disabilities

Despite the fears of employers, the accommodations actually required for individuals with ADD or LD are generally not expensive or extensive. The President's Committee on Employment for People with Disabilities has concluded that:

-- 31% of accommodations cost nothing
-- 50% cost less than $50
-- 69% cost less then $500
-- 88% cost less than $1,000

Certainly, in many cases, job retraining costs much more than the accommodations necessary to keep a valued employee.

Specific Sample Work Accommodations for People With ADD/LD

** Employees with ADD need structure. ADD adults are often successful in the military because there is a high level of structure provided.

** Pressure often disorganizes the ADD employee. Give them enough time to do their job, without undue pressure.

** Use praise more than threats. Threats and anger trigger off negative memories in the past for most ADD people. An employer is likely to get much more productivity from the ADD employee by using praise and encouragement.

** Help with organization. ADD employees often have serious problems with organization. Teaching them effective ways to organize their work area and time may help them significantly.

** Give simple instructions and have the employee repeat them back. As I've mentioned, people with ADD may only process 30% of what is said. It is critical to check with them to ensure they understand what is expected of them.

** Modify hiring tests and on-the-job performance tests. People with ADD often need more time to complete tests to show what they really know. Employers could lose a valuable asset by excluding someone based on timed tests. In a similar way, on-the-job performance tests need to be modified so that the ADD person is not at a disadvantage.

** Supplement verbal instructions with visual instructions.

** Adjust work schedules when possible. Many people with ADD have trouble getting up early in the morning and do better with work schedules which begin later in the day. Also, provide a grace period for tardiness and have the employee, when late, be able to make up time at the end of the day (as long as this won't interfere with the behavior or morale of other employees).

Other suggestions from Carol Means, Ed.D of the Job Accommodations Network at West Virginia University include:

Computer related:

word processing programs with spell checkers and grammar checkers;
software organizers, such as those by Borland, Micro Logic and Micro Systems
software flow charts
computer screen reading systems/reading machines

Clerical:

color coding
color templates
electronic and desktop organizers,
          such as those by Casio, Franklin and Sharp
cassette recorders
telephone recorders/adapter switches
dictaphones
audio prompts/cue cards
electronic spelling masters

Memory aids:

personal assistant devices
timers, counters
Neuropage

Time management skills:

goal setting
staying on one task until it is finished

Managing the physical environment:

mapping
room enclosures

tinnitus maskers/environmental sound machines

For more information contact the Job Accommodation Network's toll free number at (800) 526-7234 or (800) ADA-WORK. Person's calling from Canada may call (800) 526-2262.

CHAPTER 31

Getting Up/Going To Bed
How ADD Affects Waking and Sleep Cycles

Getting up in the morning and going to sleep at night can be real problems for people with ADD. Sleep and waking problems are very common with this disorder.

Getting Up

Mornings can be the worst. Here are some common statements people with ADD say as they're trying to get out of bed:

"Later..."
"Just a few more minutes."
"I'll get up in a little bit."
"Leave me alone."
"My alarm is set." (even though it already went off)
"I'm too tired to get up."
"OK, I'm up." (only to lay back down for several hours)

Many people with ADD feel very groggy or fuzzy headed in the morning. The harder they try to get out of bed, the worse it gets. One teenager I know had such a hard time getting out of bed that she almost got fired from her summer job. Her boss told her if she was late one more time she was gone. She had three alarm clocks and she had two of her friends call her in the morning. Many high school students have difficulty being late for school because of the trouble getting up. Adults with ADD also have this problem. Have you ever heard of adults who say that they have to have a couple of cups of coffee in the morning to get going? Coffee contains the stimulant caffeine (stimulants are common treatment for ADD).

Parents complain that they have to wake up ADD children and teenagers 3, 4, 5, 6, even 10 times before they get out of bed. This can cause a lot of family turmoil in the morning. When parents have to tell a child over and over to get out of bed, they can get pretty irritable. They may start yelling, threatening, or using force to get the child moving. Some parents we know use water or ice to help the child or teen get up. The morning grogginess causes many people with ADD to be frequently late, which stresses out everyone in the morning, especially if the parent has to get to work or has other children to get to school.

The child or teen who is awakened by the parent's hostility starts the day off in a bad mood. It's hard to concentrate in class when you have just been yelled at, threatened, or grounded because you couldn't get out of bed on time. This also leads to other problems. For example, if you can't get up on time, you may miss the bus, get a speeding ticket, end up in the tardy tank, or just cut class so that you're not late again. Starting the day off on the wrong foot can affect your mood and attitude for the whole day.

Many ADD people say that when they get up on their own, they tend to do better than if someone is screaming at them to get out of bed. It often becomes a battle of wills, because the person is angry that someone is nagging them. Both people end up feeling terrible.

Without parents hassling kids, some children and teenagers don't get out of bed until noon, 1, 2 or even 3 PM. This can cause serious problems. When kids get up late, they will have trouble going to sleep at night. Getting up late causes a large part of the day to go by without participating in it. Many parents complain that their kids are wasting the day.

Helpful Hints For Getting Going In The A.M.

1. Go to bed at a reasonable time (see bedtime suggestions below).

2. Find an alarm clock that plays the kind of music that gets the person going (some people like fast rock music to wake them up, others like rap, some even like country music). Try different forms of music to see what works best. This beats having someone else stressed out. (You know stressed out people often take it out on others.)

3. Keep the alarm clock (or clocks) across the room so that the person has to get

out of bed to turn it off. Don't have the kind of alarm that turns itself off after 30 seconds. Have one that keeps going, and going, and going.

4. Take your medicine a half hour before you're supposed to get out of bed.

5. Have something for the ADD person to do that motivates him or her in the morning. Sometimes having a girlfriend or boyfriend call you can be great motivation. Some people enjoy working out with weights in the morning as a way to get their bodies (and brains) feeling alive.

6. Stay away from early classes and early morning jobs if possible. In college, many of my patients don't start class until after 10:00 a.m. Being late irritates teachers and bosses, which is the last thing someone wants to do if he or she want to do well in school or in a job!)

7. Watch the body's own cycle. Some people are good in the morning and some later on. Fit your schedule to your body's rhythms.

Going To Bed

Many people with ADD have sleep problems. Some "go and go" all day until they drop from exhaustion. Others have difficulty getting asleep, they wake up frequently throughout the night, or they're hyper in their sleep and constantly on the move. The person who gets a restful night's sleep is more likely to be calmer in the morning. The ADD person, who is often very hard to wake up anyway, becomes even more difficult to wake up in the morning and is certainly more irritable with a poor night's sleep.

Here are some of the things people with ADD have said about their sleep problems:

"I have to count sheep to get to sleep. The stupid sheep are always talking to me."

"When I try to get to sleep all kinds of different thoughts come into my mind. It feels like my mind spins when I try to calm it down."

"I feel so restless at night. It's hard to settle down, even though I'm tired."

"The worries from the day go over and over in my head. I just can't shut my brain down."

"I have to sleep with a fan to drown out my thoughts. I need noise to calm down."

Sleep problems can cause many other problems. When you don't get enough sleep, you're tired in the morning, making it even harder to get up (which is already a problem for people with ADD). If it is hard to settle down at night, it might make parents mad (because they know too well about the morning problems) and cause fighting between the parent and child. Not getting enough sleep continues the cycle of feeling tired and wanting to sleep during the day.

One teenager I know had such trouble sleeping that he could never go to bed before three o'clock in the morning. This caused terrible problems because he couldn't get up in the morning and he had to drop out of school. This caused him to feel isolated from other people his age. He even went to the Stanford University Sleep Center for help with his problem. In the end, medication was needed to help his sleep cycle.

Doctors aren't sure why people with ADD have more sleep problems. Some doctors think it has to do with a brain chemical called serotonin. When there is not enough of this sleep chemical is more of a problem.

12 Ways To Get To Sleep

Here are ten ways to increase your serotonin and make it easier to go to sleep. No one suggestion will work for everyone, but keep trying new tactics until you find what works for your situation:

1. Eliminate television 1 - 2 hours before bedtime, especially any program that may be overstimulating (the shows you most like). This includes news programs, as people with ADD tend to ruminate on the bad things that happened that day in their own world and the world at large.

2. Stimulating, active play should be eliminated for 1 - 2 hours before bedtime, such as wrestling, tickling, teasing, etc. Quiet activities are more helpful in the

hours before bedtime, such as reading, drawing, or writing.

3. Some people try to read themselves to sleep. This can be helpful. But read boring books. If you read action-packed thrillers or horror stories you're not likely to drift off into peaceful never-never land

4. A warm, quiet bath is often helpful.

5. A bedtime back rub in bed may be soothing. Starting from the neck and working down in slow rhythmic strokes can be very relaxing. Some children and teens say that a foot massage is particularly helpful (although it may be hard to find someone to give a teen a foot massage if they haven't showered or taken a bath before bed).

6. Soft, slow music often helps people drift off to sleep. Instrumental music, as opposed to vocal, seems to be the most helpful. Some people with ADD say that they need fast music in order to block out their thoughts. Use what works.

7. Nature sounds tapes (rain, thunder, ocean, rivers) can be very helpful. Others like the sound of fans.

8. Some people with ADD say that restrictive bedding is helpful, such as a sleeping bag or being wrapped tightly in blankets.

9. A mixture of warm milk, a tablespoon of vanilla (not imitation vanilla, the real stuff), and a tablespoon of sugar can be very helpful. This increases serotonin to your brain and helps you sleep.

10. I make a sleep tape in my office with a special sound machine that produces sound waves at the same frequency as a sleeping brain. The tape is played at bedtime and helps the brain "tune in" to a brain wave sleep state, which encourages a peaceful sleep.

11. Learn self-hypnosis. Self-hypnosis can be a powerful tool for many different reasons, including sleep. Here's a quick self-hypnosis course:

-- focus your eyes on a spot and count slowly to 20...let your eyes feel heavy as you count and close them as you get to 20.

-- take three or four very slow, deep breaths

-- tighten the muscles in your arms and legs and then let them relax.

-- imagine yourself walking down a staircase while you count backwards from 10 (this will give you the feeling of "going down" or becoming sleepy)

-- with all of your senses (sight, touch, hearing, taste, smelling) imagine a very sleepy scene, such as by a fire in a mountain cabin or in a sleeping bag at the beach.

12. Sometimes medications are needed if getting to sleep is a chronic problem. There are pros and cons to using medication sleep aids. On the positive side, medications tends to work quickly and can help normalize a disturbed sleep pattern. On the negative side, medications can have side effects (such as grogginess in the morning) and you can become dependent on them if you take them for too long. It is best to think of medications for sleeping problems as a short term solution. Use the other ideas first.

The different medications doctors prescribe to help promote sleep include:

Over-the-counter medications (you can get these medications without a prescription): such as Benadryl, Unisom, Sominex, Execdrin PM, Nyquil, etc.

Some antidepressants, such as imipramine (Tofranil), amitrityline (Elavil), or trazodone (Desyrel) (trazodone is used only in females; in men it may cause painful erections that won't go away). Often these are used in very low doses to help promote sleep. They are helpful in people who have a tendency toward depression.

Certain blood pressure medications such as clonidine (Catapres). Clonidine is often used to calm down the restlessness or hyperactivity that often goes along with ADD.

Sleeping medications, such as temazepam (Restoril), triazolam (Halcion), zolpidem (Ambien), flurazepam (Dalman), estazolam (ProSom). These medications tend to lose their effectiveness after a few weeks. They should be used on a short term basis only.

Getting up and going to sleep can hinder the success of a person with ADD. Use the techniques in this chapter to help. Be persistent. If one technique doesn't work for you, don't give up...try others.

CHAPTER 32

Reprogramming Your Thoughts For Success

Many people with ADD have been programmed or in a sense "hypnotized" into believing they can't change the problems that are holding them back from being successful in their lives. This negative belief system is the first thing that must change before anything else can. Here are a set of instructions to make your own (or for your child) self-hypnotic tape to change the negative emotional tapes playing in your head.

1. Use a tape recorder that will clearly record your voice. Use your voice on the tape. Change is going to occur within you; get used to listening to your own voice. (A parent's voice is often soothing and acceptable to a child. If you are doing this for your child, modify the instructions as appropriate.)

2. When you first begin taping, record your full name (use a name the child chooses). Use your name often in the tape.

3. Tell yourself to sit in a comfortable chair, loosen all tight clothing, and let yourself feel relaxed all over.

4. Then, tell yourself to pick a spot on the wall, a little above your eye level, and stare at it. As you do, count slowly to twenty. When you get to 6, 12, and 18 tell yourself to feel the heaviness in your eyelids. And when you get to twenty, tell yourself to slowly let your eyelids close. If you find your eyes wandering, that's O.K., just bring them back to stare at the spot.

5. Next, on the tape, tell yourself to take three deep breaths, each time exhaling very slowly. Say, "with each breath in I just breath in relaxation, and with each breath out I just blow out all the tension, all the things that interfere with my becoming as relaxed as possible."

6. After that, tell yourself to tightly squeeze the muscles in your eyelids:

"Close your eyes as tightly as you can. And then, slowly let the muscles in your eyelids relax. Notice how much more they have relaxed." Then progressively tell yourself to imagine that relaxation spreading from the muscles in your eyelids, to the muscles in your face---down your neck into your shoulders and arms---into your chest and throughout the rest of your body. The muscles will take the relaxation cue from your eyelids and relax progressively all the way down to the bottom of your feet. Some like to imagine themselves in a warm tub, some liken their relaxed muscles to a limp wet rag. Use what works for you.

7. Next on the tape, describe a place where you feel comfortable, your special haven so to speak, a place that you can imagine with all of your senses. Your haven can be a real or imagined place. It can be any place where you'd like to spend time. Describe it on the tape, using all of your senses, in as much detail as possible (for children ask them ahead of time; they often like the beach, mountains or a beautiful park). Then say, "As you listen to the rest of the tape, imagine yourself walking in your haven, looking and exploring its inner reaches."

-- These first few steps should take about 5 - 10 minutes.

8. After you go through these initial steps, read the following phrases into the tape recorder (modify to better suit your own, (or your child's, situation):

"Now that I feel very relaxed, and very comfortable...I feel physically stronger and fitter in every way. With each breath in, I just breath in strength...and with each breath out, I blow out the tensions and weaknesses that hold me back. Day-by-day, I feel more in control of my life...more able to do what I enjoy doing, rather than what other people think I should be doing. I develop my own goals and focus my energy on them. I know deep down what makes me happy, where I belong...I now have the strength to follow through with my dreams.

"I expect to succeed at whatever I set out to do...and I see myself succeeding before my effort...I program myself for success. That doesn't mean that there won't be failures. Everyone fails at one time or another -- everyone...expecting myself to be perfect is not practical. On the other hand, I will learn from my failures...and become a better person every day. No longer will I have to make the same mistakes over and over. I learn from the mistakes and move on. I also strive to learn from others...we live in a relational, teaching world...and I am a willing pupil. Acting like a know-it-all does not help me in any way...learning from others always has the potential for expanding my horizons.

"In a similar way I am a more informed person...When I have questions, I ask them. I am always on the lookout for new and different information. I prepare for my tasks, setting myself up to win, instead of putting off my tasks and setting myself up to fail. Organization is becoming more second nature to me...I realize that when I put something in its right place initially, I'm more likely to find it when I need it.

"Making decisions is easier for me. I ask the right questions, gather good information before deciding on it, talk to those affected by the decision to get their input, see my options, and then decide on the thing based on the goals I have for myself. I am thus able to take reasonable risks, while being able to avoid taking risks that are dangerous for me.

"Every day I strive to become more focused, more alert, more wide awake and more energetic. I am becoming much less easily tired, much less easily fatigued, much less easily discouraged, much less easily depressed and much less easily anxious. Every day I am more deeply interested in what I'm doing, in whatever is going on around me and in the people around me. I work smart as well as hard, focusing my energy on the goals I have set for myself. I am also more observant of situations and people around me, truly seeing what is there to see and listening to what I hear.

"Starting now, I am able to look at common things in uncommon ways. I act and think more creatively. No longer do I have to solve problems in unproductive ways of the past. Creativity is not the prerogative of artists, it is part of all humans...I do not have to stay in any rut, unless I choose to stay in it. Day-by-day I am also more flexible...more adaptable...more willing to change as change is needed. At the same time, I am more disciplined...less impulsive...I keep the words, "Thinking Is Trial Action," in the front of my brain, and refer to them every time I wish to do something that may not be in my best interest.

"I realize now that, in part, I am a product of my environment...If my environment is negative, so am I. I teach others, by my actions, that they need to treat me with respect, and in turn, I treat them as I wish to be treated. I also spend time with those who uplift me and believe in me. I surround myself with positive people. On the same note, I focus my energy on being more empathetic with those around me. I am now able to get outside of myself to understand the feelings of others...and I am willing to see things from their perspective as well as from my own. No longer am I afraid of competing with others...it is great when I win...but I can learn new things from any situation. Competition spurs me on to be as good as I can be.

"With ever-increasing frequency, I accept myself and others as we are, instead of how I think things should be. I compromise when necessary...and I now refuse to let the accusing inner voices have free reign over how I feel about myself. I am in control of me...and I live with inner voices that help and uplift me, rather than ones that try to tear me down. I fight the negative voices within whenever they appear.

"Gradually, I find less and less need to worry about future problems and dangers, many of which are quite imaginary and silly when I really think about them. I am increasingly able to determine the real dangers about the things I fear and to determine the reasonable probabilities of their occurrence. Most of the things we worry about never happen...I am now able to mobilize my anxieties into energy by preparing for the other tasks I need to do, thus decreasing my overall anxiety. Every day, I find myself successful in overcoming the anxiety that holds me back.

"Every day, the irrationalities of the past influence my life less and less. I reject the idea that the traumas of the past need to have powerful importance in my life. I live in the present...I have choices in the present. My life is not dictated by what happened when I was young...I can overcome the past, excess baggage that has been weighing me down.

"I never give up on myself. I give my best effort toward reaching the goals I have set for myself, and no matter what, I keep pursuing the dreams in my life. I am flexible enough to change as change is needed, but I believe in my ability and I never give up on me."

9. Now, on the tape, tell yourself to count backwards from ten, and as you do say that you will feel more awake, more alert, and full of energy to do whatever you wish to do. When you get to zero, open your eyes, stretch, and get up and walk around the room.

The total time of the tape will be from 10 - 25 minutes, depending on the pace of your voice, images, and so on.

Now that you have made the tape for yourself or your child, listen to it once every day. It is important, the first few times you listen to the tape, that you find out how your body will react to the relaxation. Some people become so relaxed that they doze off to sleep for a bit. If that happens to you, great! Listen to the tape before you go to bed, or when you can catch a nap. Some people find that it takes them a while to be fully with it; they remain very relaxed for several minutes afterward, as if they were waking up from sleep. If the tape affects you that way, you want to make sure that you're clearly awake before you do anything that requires full concentration, like driving a car. Others can listen to the tape anytime, anywhere, and feel a relaxed energy flow through their body.

The most important thing is that you listen to your tape every day. You can change the content of the tape in any way that you think will be beneficial to you. This is your tape. Use it to strengthen your life.

CHAPTER 33

Advantages Of ADD

Is there anything good about having ADD? Yes!! Many people with ADD have wonderful traits and abilities that often get overlooked.

Here's a list:

•Flexibility: many children, teens and adults with ADD are flexible, and they may be able to adapt to different situations.

•Intelligent: even though they don't feel like it, many people with ADD are very smart.

•Creative: many people with ADD are able to see traditional things in untraditional ways. They can often come up with new ideas or solutions for difficult situations.

•Intuitive: many people with ADD have good intuition and they are able to relate with people who struggle.

•High energy and spontaneous: many people with ADD have a lot of energy, they are able to "live in the moment," be spontaneous, and they are fun to be around.

•Lots of ideas: many people with ADD have lots and lots of ideas. In business, they are successful if they can surround themselves with people who help them organize their ideas.

With proper diagnosis and treatment, ADD is a highly treatable disorder. Without proper diagnosis, serious problems are common in many areas of an ADD person's life.

MindWorks Press
Books/Audios/Videos by
Daniel G. Amen, M.D.
2220 Boynton Ave, Suite C, Fairfield, CA 94533
707.429.7181 Fax 707.429.8210

Windows Into The A.D.D. Mind: Attention Deficit Disorders in Children, Teens and Adults

Book: A comprehensive guide to everything you need to know about ADD in children, teenagers, and adults. Includes case studies, diagnostic checklists, subtypes of ADD, brain images, specific suggestions on medication management, individual and family therapy techniques, organizational strategies, and many other ideas for living with ADD at home, school, and work..$39.95_____

Brain Train Enhancement Tapes: (2 tapes) Made with a special sound machine these tapes produce sound waves at frequencies that help your brain either focus or relax...................................$29.95_____

Self-Hypnosis: (1 tape) Self-hypnotic reprogramming for negative thoughts associated with ADD.......................$14.95_____

Medications For ADD: Audio: (2 tapes) the latest information on the use of ,medications for ADD, including the use of combination medications..$29.95_____

Complete ADD Audio Set: (8 tapes) Live seminar on all aspects of ADD. Also included, "ADD and Medication" tapes, "Brain Train" tapes, and "Self-hypnosis for ADD" tape.......................................$89.95_____

Set Discounts!!
Windows Book/Video $79.95
Windows Book/Compete Audio Set $99.95
Windows Book/Complete Audio Set and Video $139.95

A.D.D. In Intimate Relationships

Audio: (2 tapes) all about the impact and healing of relationships touched by ADD.......................................$29.95_____

A Teenager's Guide To A.D.D.

Book: A complete guide to A.D.D. for teenagers, including tips on medication, getting along with others at home, school, and work, homework, driving, and intimate relationships....................................$29.95_____

Healing The Chaos Within:

The Interaction Between A.D.D., Alcoholism, and Growing Up In An Alcoholic Home

Audio/Workbook Program: Includes a 1 hr audiotape and workbook with checklists, questionnaires on ADD, Alcoholism, and Adult Children of Alcoholics. The interaction between these 3 conditions is explained and specific interventions are given for healing the chaos these disorders bring to individuals and families.....................$29.95_____

New Skills For Frazzled Parents

Book: Includes real stories, handouts, charts, tips, home and school behavior systems..$29.95_____

Audio Series: (8 tapes) 8 full hours of a complete parent training course taught by Dr. Amen.

Step-by-step instructions on superior parenting difficult and not-so-difficult children and teens................................$89.95_____

Video: (1 hour 20 min) Dr. Amen LIVE on parenting difficult kids with humor, and practical advice............................$49.95_____

Set Discounts!! ☞ ☞ ☞   Book/Audios........$99.95_____

Book/Video...........$74.95_____

The Complete Set of Book/Audios/Video................................☆$139.95_____

Don't Shoot Yourself In The Foot: A Program To End Self-Defeating Behavior Forever

Book: Includes self-diagnostic quizzes, checklists, exercises, goal sheets, hallmarks of self-defeating and

successful behavior, actions and thoughts. Also, instructions on making personalized change self-hypnosis tape..............$11.99_____

Audio Series: (2 tapes) 2 hours of Dr. Amen LIVE on Don't Shoot Yourself In The Foot....................................$29.95_____

Video: (1 hour 20 min) Dr. Amen LIVE on eight prescriptions for success...$49.95_____

Set Discounts!! ☞ ☞ ☞   Book/Audios.....$37.95_____

Book/Video........$54.95_____

The Complete Set of Book/Audios/Video....................$79.95_____

The Most Important Thing In Life I Learned From A Penguin!?

A Story On How To Help People Change. Illustrated by Breanne L. Amen

Book: 23 illustrations, plus a second "real life" penguin fable...$12.95_____

Would You Give *TWO MINUTES A DAY* For A Lifetime Of Love

Book: Total Focus is needed to keep marriages young and alive. This book teaches you how to achieve total

focus in your relationship and it gives you the skills to make it happen...$19.95_____

Audio: (2 Tapes, 100 min) Dr. Amen LIVE, teaching couples how to achieve total focus in their relationships.............$29.95_____

Video: (1 hour 20 min) Dr. Amen LIVE on achieving TOTAL FOCUS for relationships...$49.95_____

Set Discounts!! ☞ ☞ ☞   Book/Audios...........$39.95_____

Book/Video.............$64.95_____

The Complete Set of Book/Audios/Video....................$89.95_____

Making The Grade: Achieving Academic Excellence

Book: The skills students need to be successful at school. For 6th graders through graduate school. Includes

chapters on organization, getting the most out of teachers, test-taking, homework, writing and speaking skills

and much more!...$29.95_____

MindCoach: How To Teach Kids and Teenagers To Think Positively and Feel Good

Book: Everything starts and ends in your mind. MindCoach teaches children and teens how to correct

the negative thought patterns which interfere with their lives. It also teaches them how to think in ways that

enhance their chances for success in whatever they do..$19.95_____

Audio: (2 Tapes, 90 min) Dr. Amen LIVE, teaching children how to think positively and feel good............................$19.95_____

Set Discount!! ☞ ☞ ☞   Book/Audios........$34.95_____

Intimate Parent-Child Talk:

What Every 8 to 16-Year-Old MUST Know Growing Up In The 90s (For Boys and Girls)

Video (2 hrs): This program is meant to be watched together by parents or group leaders and their pre-teen or teenage children. Includes nine talks (approx 10 min each) between a father and his 12-year-old son about the things parents should tell their kids, but never do. Topics covered include peer pressure, normal sexual development, teenage pregnancy, AIDS, drugs, and decision making..$59.95_____

Ten Steps To Building Values Within Children

Audio/Workbook Program: Includes a 1 hr. audiotape and workbook, giving parents 10 steps to building values within children. Never before are values such an issue in our society. Parents need the best information and this program gives you step-by-step guidelines..$29.95_____

Smoke Stop: A Self-Hypnosis And Behavioral Change Program To End Smoking Forever

Audio/Workbook: This program includes an audiocassette explaining the **Smoke Stop** program. A hypnotic audiotape, recorded live, for **Smoke Stop**. A 66 page workbook for **Smoke Stop**. *Special Bonus:* Two special recordings made with a sound machine that stimulates brain activity; one to enhance concentration, one for relaxation.......$49.95_____

Images Into The Mind: A Radical New Look At Understanding And Changing Behavior

Audio/Book: Brain SPECT Imaging is changing the way we view psychiatric illness. Dr. Amen has been at the forefront of brain imaging research. In this program he shares specific brain patterns which correlate with certain psychiatric conditions (depression, ADD, anxiety, obsessive-compulsive disorder, violence, etc. In addition, based on his research he offers clear prescriptions for healing the mind. Includes a one-hour audiotape and a 250 page book with 39 SPECT images..$49.95_____

Images Into The Mind: The Video (90 minutes)

Do you think you know why people do what they do? Your opinion may change after watching this video. Utilizing some of the most sophisticated brain imaging technology in medicine, Dr. Daniel Amen will give you an intimate look into a "working brain." Based on his brain imaging work with over 1500 patients, Dr. Amen will teach you the functions of the major systems of the brain (limbic system, basal ganglia, prefrontal cortex, cingulate gyrus, and temporal lobes), and graphically show what happens when things go wrong. He will correlate different brain patterns with specific feeling and behavior states, along with certain psychiatric disorders. Case studies (along with the colorized images) will be given to show you how this work translates into everyday clinical practice..$69.95_____

Buy A Library of Dr. Amen's Materials And Save Over $200.00!!

The total for all products (except Clinician's Guide To ADD), using set discounts, is over $800. We would like to offer you the complete library for only: $600 (S&H included free). With a purchase of $200 or more, the Clinicians Guide To ADD Series may be purchased for $100 off at $199.95.

A New 5 Hour Video/Workbook Series On A.D.D. For Clinicians

By Daniel G. Amen, M.D.

Understanding And Treating Attention Deficit Disorders
(Childhood Through Adulthood)
A Comprehensive Step-By-Step Guide for Clinicians

VIDEO SERIES TOPICS

Understanding A.D.D.
(with and without hyperactivity)

○ A.D.D. throughout the life cycle: real stories
○ The prevalence across the life cycle in males and females (why girls are rarely diagnosed)
○ Checklists of A.D.D. in children, teenagers and adults (those by Dr. Amen will be included in the handouts)
○ Five Subtypes of A.D.D. with specific medication and psychotherapeutic recommendations for each.
○ Impact of A.D.D. on school, work, relationships, and self-esteem.

Diagnosing A.D.D.
(from beginning to end)

○ Brain imaging and A.D.D. with actual case studies to illustrate subtypes
○ Psychological testing and A.D.D.
○ Differentiating A.D.D. from depression, bipolar disorders, anxiety disorders, personality disorders, and substance abuse.
○ Making the diagnosis
○ Communicating the diagnosis in a way that enhances treatment compliance for patients and families

Effectively Treating A.D.D.
(specific strategies)

○ Family therapy
○ Sibling issues
○ Specific school interventions
○ Parent training
○ Anger management
○ Work accommodations
○ Medications (the latest information on the use of stimulants, serotonergic meds such as Prozac and combination therapies)
○ Psychotherapeutic interventions

Understanding the Law and A.D.D.

○ PL 94-142
○ Section 504
○ Americans with Disabilities Act.

Building A Thriving A.D.D. Practice
(step-by-step)

○ How you will benefit in this practice
○ How to build an A.D.D. practice
○ Who to contact, who to meet,

WORKBOOK TOPICS

Intake Forms/Questionnaires
(from Dr. Amen's own clinic)

- Child/Teenager Intake Questionnaires, including extensive Parent Questionnaire (great history taking tool)
- Child/Teenager Checklists, including DSM-IV Criteria for A.D.D., *checklists for subtypes of A.D.D.*, checklists for Depression, Anxiety Disorders, Oppositional Defiant Disorder and Conduct Disorder
- Child/Teenager Mental Status Form, including instructions for performing screening for soft neurological signs
- Extensive Adult Intake Questionnaire (great history taking tool)
- Adult Symptoms Checklist, includes checklists for Depression, Bipolar, Panic, Generalized Anxiety, Obsessive-Compulsive, and Post Traumatic Stress Disorders, Agoraphobia, Eating Disorders, Tourette's and Temporal Lobe Symptoms
- Adult ADD Symptom Checklist (77 questions)
- Adult Mental Status Exam, includes brain functions by lobes

Brain Anatomy And Function Relating To A.D.D.
(special section)

- Functions and problems of the brain's limbic system, basal ganglia, cingulate system and prefrontal cortex
- Psychotherapeutic recommendations for healing specific parts of the mind, including limbic system, basal ganglia, cingulate system and prefrontal cortex exercises

Brain Imaging and A.D.D.
- Journal abstracts on brain imaging and A.D.D.
- Dr. Amen's book chapter on Brain SPECT Imaging

Medication and A.D.D.
- Common questions and answers on medications for A.D.D., including helpful combinations
- Instructions for starting stimulants
- Monthly progress rating sheets, office follow-up sheets
- Patient information sheets for medications used for A.D.D.

Testing, Teaching, Parenting and A.D.D.
- List of psychological tests for A.D.D., including rating scales, tests for vigilance, sustained attention and impulsiveness
- Strategies for helping A.D.D. students
- Typical methods for modifying academic tasks
- Daily Report Card system for school
- Successful parenting strategies for difficult children

Adult A.D.D. Interventions
- Psychotherapeutic techniques for A.D.D. adults
- Anger management strategies
- Killing the A.N.T.s Exercise (exterminating the Automatic Negative Thoughts associated with A.D.D.)

Popular Articles and A.D.D.
- Popular articles you can copy and handout to clients
- A list of famous people with A.D.D. or learning dis abilities

The Law and A.D.D.
- Summaries of Public Law 94-142, DOE Section 504, and the Americans with Disabilities Act
- Sample work accommodations for people with A.D.D.
- A List of references and legal advocates

The 5 Hour Video Series and Workbook
FOR ONLY $299.95

Understanding And Treating Attention Deficit Disorders
(Childhood Through Adulthood)
A Comprehensive Step-By-Step Guide for Clinicians

◆Dr. Amen received a standing ovation from over 1,000 attendees at the National Adult A.D.D. Conference May '94 in Ann Arbor, Michigan. His programs are uniformly ranked as superior, practical and fun.

◆Cogent, coherent, informative, engaging. An outstanding presentation!
-- Jerry Jones, M.D., Psychiatrist, Stockton, CA

◆Wonderful! A perfect overview for clinicians.
-- Phijoc V. Nguyen, Ph.D., San Joaquin Mental Health Center

◆Outstanding overall presentation for professionals.
-- Brad Berman, M.D., Child Neurologist/Psychiatrist, Children's Hospital, Oakland, CA

◆The biology of ADD was excellent!
-- Gib Eggen, D.O., Psychiatrist, Turlock, CA

◆Excellent! A must have for every clinician!!
-- Tianna Nelson, Public Defender's Office, Santa Rosa, CA

◆Great overview, assessment tools. Interesting, informative!
-- Marlene Woertz, MFCC, Napa, CA

◆Excellent!! Best I've heard, including Barkley and Goldstein. I learned a lot in a very short period of time!
-- Frank Varella, Ph.D., Napa State Hospital, CA

◆Excellent!! Dr. Amen presented from the heart and from the head. He manages to communicate on a very serious subject that can devastate individuals and families. Yet he is funny and filled with compassion as well.
-- Cynthia Kessler, Ph.D., Psychologist

◆This is great stuff! It's important on many levels. We need more presentations like this one to get the information out there.
-- Candice Trudeau, Ph.D., Psychologist

◆Outstanding!! The parent training tips were very helpful.
-- Robert Picker, MD, Psychiatrist, Walnut Creek, CA

Order Form

☎ **Telephone orders:** Toll Free: (800) 626-2700 ext 400.   Have your Visa, Amex, MasterCard ready   (24hrs)

* **Fax orders:** (707) 429-8210 (24 hours a day)

▭ **Postal orders:** Daniel G. Amen, M.D., 2220 Boynton Ave., Suite C, Fairfield, CA 94533 (707) 429-7181

Please send the following products. I understand that I may return any product within 30 days for a full refund -- for any reason, no questions asked.

_____
_____
_____
_____
_____
_____
_____
_____
_____

Sub-total	_____
Shipping/Handling (10%)	_____
Sales Tax: Please add 7.25% for book shipped to a California address	_____
Total Enclosed	_____

Name:_____

Address:_____

City:_____State:_____Zip:_____-_____Phone: _____

Payment: ❑ **Check**   ❑ **Credit card:**   ❑**Visa,** ❑**MasterCard,** ❑**Amex**

Card number:_____

Name on card:_____**Exp. date:** _____/_____

Daniel G. Amen, M.D.
Psychiatrist, Author, Lecturer

Daniel G. Amen, M.D. is a nationally recognized expert in the field of Attention Deficit Disorder. He has been the key note speaker at many national adult A.D.D. conferences. He has presented his ground breaking research on brain imaging and A.D.D. across the country. The Discovery Channel did a special feature on his brain imaging work in the field of psychiatry.

Dr. Amen is a board certified child, adolescent and adult psychiatrist and the medical director of a large, innovative A.D.D. clinic in Fairfield, CA. He has evaluated and treated over 3000 patients with A.D.D. Patients come to his clinic from around the country, and as far away as West Africa.

Dr. Amen's wife and two of his three children have A.D.D. He understands the frustrations of dealing with difficult children, dealing with difficult school systems, and dealing with therapists who unknowingly do more harm than good when they don't understand A.D.D. Perhaps one of his greatest strengths is that he can speak about this disorder from a personal, as well as a professional perspective.

Dr. Amen did his psychiatric training at Walter Reed Army Medical Center in Washington, D.C. He has won writing and research awards from the American Psychiatric Association, the Baltimore-D.C. Institute for Psychoanalysis and the U.S. Army. Dr. Amen has been published around the world. He is the author of over 250 articles, eight books, and a number of audio and video programs.

Dr. Amen has appeared in the media across the country, including television appearances on the Discovery Channel, The Geraldo Show and CNN's Sonya Live, along with over 150 radio appearances. Additionally, Dr. Amen has been quoted by the Wall Street Journal, the Associated Press, the San Francisco Chronicle and the Atlanta Journal Constitution.

Keynotes and Seminars

IMAGES INTO THE MIND
A Radical New Look At
Understanding and Changing Behavior

WINDOWS INTO THE A.D.D. MIND
Understanding and Treating Attention Deficit
Disorders, Childhood Through Adulthood

HEALING THE CHAOS WITHIN
The Interaction Between ADD, Alcoholism and
Growing Up In An Alcoholic Home

THE INTERFERENCE OF A.D.D. AT WORK
Identification And Interventions
of A.D.D. At Work

OVERCOMING THE INTIMACY GAP
Healing ADD In Relationships

WOULD YOU GIVE 2 MINUTES A DAY FOR A LIFETIME OF LOVE

DON'T SHOOT YOURSELF IN THE FOOT
A Program To End Self Defeating Behavior Forever
(in relationships, at work, and individually)

MAKING THE GRADE
A Step-By-Step Guide To Success In School

RUNNING FULL SPEED INTO A BRICK WALL
Managing Time and Stress in the 90s

NEW SKILLS FOR FRAZZLED PARENTS
Developing Superior Parenting Skills for Diffiult Kids

MINDCOACH FOR KIDS
Teaching Children and Teenagers to
Think Positive and Feel Good

AN INTIMATE PARENT-CHILD TALK
What Every Child and Teen Must Know Growing Up

**For information call (707) 429-7181 or write to
2220 Boynton Ave, Suite C, Fairfield, CA 94533**